9/2016

The Courage Solution

The Power of Truth Telling
with Your Boss, Peers, and Team

THE

COURAGE

SOLUTION

MINDY MACKENZIE

GREENLEAF
BOOK GROUP PRESS
www.gbgpress.com

Names have been changed unless specific permission to use
them has been granted by the individual.

Published by Greenleaf Book Group Press
Austin, Texas
www.gbgpress.com

Distributed by Greenleaf Book Group.
For ordering information or special discounts for bulk purchases,
please contact Greenleaf Book Group at PO Box 91869, Austin, TX
78709, 512.891.6100.

Copyediting by Judy Phillips
Proofreading by Shirarose Wilensky
Jacket design by Peter Cocking
Jacket photo by ANP/Shutterstock
Interior design by Nayeli Jimenez

www.thecouragesolutionbook.com
www.mindymackenzie.com

Cataloging-in-Publication data is available.
Print ISBN: 978-1-62634-330-6
eBook ISBN: 978-1-62634-331-3

Printed and bound in Canada

16 17 18 19 20 21 10 9 8 7 6 5 4 3 2

First Edition

For Noah and John. You are my truth tellers.

And for Kevin. I love you with my whole heart.

CONTENTS

PREFACE

IN WRITING THIS book, I attempted to balance stories from my experience with stories from my colleagues. When I had completed the manuscript, my editor encouraged me to preface it by sharing my life story so that you, the reader, would know why I believe passionately in courage and truth telling. As both a 20-year veteran of human resources and a trained psychotherapist, I know that every person has a story. Each person you encounter at work, no matter how polished or together they seem, has likely experienced more heartache and trauma and challenge than you'd expect. Myself included.

This truth was reinforced several years ago at a dinner for executive team members. As we chatted, we began sharing stories of our first jobs (nearly all of us started working at age 12), the humble circumstances of our families, how we scraped through college, and so on. We drew the conclusion that there was a benefit to that early working and scraping and effort—it contributed to the degree of success and accomplishment we had achieved, since our early starts weren't what would be called "easy."

My childhood in Michigan involved prolonged, severe abuse. It was extraordinarily painful in every sense (physically, mentally, and emotionally) yet easy for others to miss because my family moved every couple of years. The benefit it did provide, however, was my obsessive desire to overcome, move on, and create a completely different experience for myself.

My solace growing up was the escape I found at school. School was a place where no one could harm me in the way I was harmed at home. I loved school. Loved studying. Loved the competitiveness of vying for the best grades. It was an environment in which I thrived, and I learned that through performing well I got the recognition I craved.

This early pattern helped me persist as I worked full time while taking full course loads at college and then graduate school. The work ethic I developed would become a cornerstone of future achievements. I have simply always loved going to work. Whether in my career as a newly minted marriage and family therapist or later as I transitioned into business, I found work to be this amazing place to get fulfillment through helping others, solving problems, and getting stuff done.

I have mentored many young people as they begin their careers and agonize over what postsecondary degrees to pursue (or what degrees they've already earned). I've always laughed and then shared that I have (1) a theology undergraduate degree and (2) a graduate degree in marriage and family therapy. Without fail, this always shocks them—which will forever amuse me. My message is that, ultimately, it doesn't matter where you went to school or what your degree is, where you come from or what your story is; what matters is what you accomplish on the job and how you contribute.

At this point in my life, I have worked for three global corporations, and I am fortunate that the first was Wal-Mart Stores, Inc. It was the quintessential meritocracy. When I joined the company in 1996, I was told to never share that I had any college education because it might be off-putting to coworkers given that many were not college educated, instead rising from the hourly-worker ranks into management. Sam Walton had built a culture where people were promoted based on results—no matter where they came from. Walmart was a place where your past was irrelevant. And given my past, I was delighted to jump in, work my tail off, and see where it went.

But I never originally envisioned a career in business, let alone in human resources. After graduate school, my plan was to head to Dallas, Texas, to join a multidisciplinary mental health practice that a group of us were forming (a psychiatrist, social worker, psychologist, and me). I felt that being a therapist was my calling, and I was driven to help people overcome their challenges and be healthier and more fulfilled. I couldn't imagine any other line of work; I considered myself a lifer. And at that point, I had never even heard of "human resources" (or "personnel," as it was then known)—or taken a business management class.

Due to unexpected circumstances, I was invited to speak to some Walmart executives as a "get to know you" exercise. When those conversations went well, after much prodding from family and friends to just "check it out and see where it goes," I interviewed at Walmart for a personnel role in the Logistics Division.

My mentor, a fellow marriage and family therapist, advised that while the practice in Dallas was being established by the others, it made sense for me to work for a year at the largest business in the world. He knew how hard it was to get a mental health practice started and profitable, and thought that at Walmart I could get terrific experience that would in turn help me help my patients, while earning good money.

My mentor's advice seemed prudent. When I accepted the role, I anticipated spending a year or so with Walmart before rejoining my therapy colleagues in Texas and settling down as a therapist—no harm, no foul.

I never made it to Dallas.

The second day on the job as the personnel manager trainee for Walmart's Transportation Office (mechanics, truck drivers, and dispatchers were now my "clients"), the woman in the top job went on medical leave. Within 48 hours of my arrival, "trainee" was dropped from my title and my orientation was over. My adventure in business had begun.

I quickly discovered that I could get the same charge out of helping people in a corporate setting as I did in a clinical setting. It was fun. And intense. And exciting. And new.

I had found my "home."

In the next nine years, I made multiple moves, which culminated with my working at headquarters and living in Bentonville, Arkansas. But while my career was flourishing, my personal life was foundering. I had had a disastrous marriage and an excruciating divorce. I was a single working mother to a beautiful baby boy—and I was ready for a change of scenery.

I toyed with the idea of going back to private practice, but before that thought had a chance to fully form, an executive search firm representing Campbell Soup Company called me. Campbell's was looking for a global organization effectiveness director to lead leadership and culture initiatives. And my experience was just what they were looking for.

When I arrived at Campbell's headquarters in Camden, New Jersey, I was no longer a starry-eyed newbie. Thanks to Walmart's prominence in the business world, I had had many priceless experiences. I was exposed to the first-rate executive teams at GE and at Motorola, worked on global projects of significant scale, facilitated five-year strategy meetings, and coached senior executives throughout the company. Bottom line? Walmart was a tremendous training ground.

I was drawn to the Campbell's job because the role afforded me the opportunity to work closely with the then CEO, Doug Conant. This was a privilege because Doug was a CEO who emphasized that successful business performance was dependent on how it was achieved. In other words, leadership and culture mattered a great deal. And my job was to partner with him to bring his vision to reality.

By the time I left Walmart, I was a firm believer that who you are as a leader either creates a tremendous positive, far-reaching impact or casts a massive shadow on the organization. That it is critical to create an environment where employees can easily do what they are hired to do. Doug walked that talk.

During my three years at headquarters, I was given positions of increasing seniority and worked on programs and initiatives that live on to this day. And I made my enthusiasm for and openness to an international role known. So when I was asked to consider the position of vice president, human resources and public affairs, for the Asia-Pacific region, my answer was a resounding yes. This was a dream job in a dream location—Sydney, Australia. I spent two years there.

The experience was full of learning experiences: what it means to run a global business, how structuring a business can make or break its results, and the importance of empowering business leaders "on the front lines" with the authority to make the calls on their business, as they are closest to the customer. None of this was theoretical. I was living it every day, all from the vantage point of the southern hemisphere.

So how did I end up at the liquor giant Jim Beam?

Again, I received an unexpected phone call from a search firm. The headhunter extolled the virtues of joining an executive team at the Chicago headquarters at the beginning of a major performance turnaround, in an industry with incredible margins and rich heritage. And I was going to be the top banana—global chief human resources officer—something I had aspired to for years.

As I contemplated this opportunity—and the fact that it would be the 18th move in my life—I wrestled with my sense of loyalty to Campbell's and my yearning to try my hand at leading from the top job. It would be an opportunity to put to the ultimate test everything I espoused about leadership and running a successful business—and the culture that requires.

Throughout my career I had experienced the effects of weak leadership. It fueled my burning desire to be in the most senior roles—I felt an obligation to do better. I felt it was my duty to lead because I knew there was a better way and that my behavior as a leader made a difference. A big difference.

So I left a company I loved, a country I felt at home in, and a happy life I had built for me and my son and uprooted once again ... with the intention of making Chicago work, no matter what happened at Jim Beam.

And oh, the things that happened at Jim Beam! Within a year of arriving, the parent, Fortune Brands, decided to break apart the company, sell off one portion, do a public spinoff of another segment, and reconstitute itself as a pure-play, stand-alone spirits company on the New York Stock Exchange. We renamed ourselves Beam, Inc. Over the next four years, we delivered 106 percent shareholder value return, before being purchased by Japanese conglomerate Suntory Holdings.

By that time, I not only had been leading human resources and communications globally but had been given strategy and corporate development as well. I'd been invited to join the board of a bank and had begun guest lecturing at Kellogg School of

Management, at Northwestern University. My son and I had settled into our community on Chicago's north shore, and our life had achieved a happy rhythm.

So how did I end up here, writing this book? Giving speeches? Working at McKinsey as a senior advisor?

It all started with a blank sheet of paper.

I had spent months with our Japanese soon-to-be owners in heavy negotiations over how the business would operate, both in the interim and after the deal closed. Given the many hats I wore, I was also intimately involved in negotiating the contracts of the executives who were choosing to stay on.

There was only one executive contract left to negotiate. Mine.

I had been deliberating about my future and whether I should stay for the next "leg of Beam's journey." The past several years had been intense, not just because of the business performance we were delivering but also because the board and CEO had begun to speak with me about my taking on larger commercial roles, and my potential as CEO. With Suntory's entrance, the game changed. And I needed to get clear on what I envisioned for my life.

I never could have imagined what transpired. A senior executive came from Japan to talk to me. Two messages were conveyed to encourage me to stay: (1) I was a legitimate candidate for the CEO spot once the incumbent moved on and (2) I could name my price.

Thus the blank sheet of paper. Literally.

My brain had trouble computing what was happening as he slid across a sheet of white paper and told me that the chairman wanted me to tell him "what it would take."

I thanked the executive profusely and asked for three days before getting back to him with my answer. The next 72 hours were truth time.

It was a fierce internal battle. My ego screamed for me to stay. My heart yearned to move forward. My head told me I'd never get another shot at the CEO spot if I turned down this one. My gut told me that if I didn't leave then, I'd regret it the rest of my life.

In the end I left.

Why?

Because I didn't want to make a difference for just one company—I wanted to make a difference for many. I didn't want to lead just a few thousand—I wanted to inspire many thousands. And most importantly, I didn't want to be just a weekend warrior parent to my son—I wanted to be truly available to the one human being who needed me around for those few more years before he left home.

Writing this book has been an endeavor of the heart and spirit, a way to pay back all the good fortune and blessings I have had in my life by sharing the most important nuggets I have learned as a leader and as a human being *so far*.

I hope that knowing my backstory inspires you on your personal and professional journey and reminds you that it really doesn't matter where you started.

INTRODUCTION
An Uncommon Approach to Leading

WHEN WAS THE last time you reclined in a comfy chair, with a delicious drink at your side, and settled in to read the latest 300-page tome on leadership?

Whenever I ask fellow members of the corporate tribe this question, they snort and sheepishly admit that they haven't cracked any book—much less a book on leadership—in a ... VERY. LONG. TIME.

Then they furtively look over their shoulder as if to check that the gods of the Corporate World haven't overheard their blasphemy.

You are not alone. Don't worry. The fact that you're reading this book is nothing short of miraculous (keeping with the mythical, pseudo-religious theme here).

When I lecture at Kellogg School of Management or give keynotes at various organizations on the topics covered in this book, professionals consistently ask for simple, practical things they can do to improve their life at work. So that is what I talk about.

Not more theories.

Not more research.

In this book, I'm sharing the handful of tools and techniques that I have found throughout my 20-year-plus career to be game-changing. This book is essentially four short books in one. It is designed so that you can read all four sections sequentially, or you can simply choose the topic area where you are wanting some practical help and go directly there. It is intended to be a just-in-time resource that you can go back to again and again. And it is organized around the four principle relationships that most impact your success in your career: the relationship you have with yourself, your boss, your peers, and those you lead. All underpinned with an uncommon philosophical twist.

I suspect that many of you readers have had unexpected peaks and valleys in your personal and professional lives. I have as well. In a nutshell, the first 17 years of my life were pretty lousy, in a scary, made-for-TV-special kind of way, and I've spent my adult life not only healing from those experiences but deliberately choosing to create a different type of life. In the process of deciding whether I was going to change or continue the patterns of the past, I came to the same conclusion about business as I did about my life: the only thing I can change is myself.

And that is the singular difference about this book. It is simple because it is based on one unalterable truth:

The only thing you can reliably control or change at your company is yourself.

Kind of annoying, isn't it? But it's true.

And we all tend to forget it.

There is a corollary that is equally as powerful:

Change is an inside-out job.

No one can do it to you or for you.

C'mon... you know this is true too.

And buying in to both of those truths takes a massive dose of courage.

This book is written from the perspective of what you can do to shift your experience—with your boss, your peers, and your direct reports so that you get more of what you want. *The Courage Solution* operates from the premise that there are straightforward, actionable things you can do to improve your impact with the people you encounter, thus improving your daily experience and dramatically increasing your joy, energy, and sense of fulfillment. *You are creating the reality you are experiencing right now*—in your life and in your career. I wrote *The Courage Solution* to inspire you to shift, so that the reality you experience is positive and beneficial for you and everyone around you.

IT TAKES COURAGE

AS YOU MAKE your way through this book, you will notice that I am going to consistently ask of you one thing: to be courageous.

Most of the tips and techniques offered up in this book require a measure of courage on your part if you choose to try them out. It is not necessary to try everything at once. In fact, a lot of what you choose to apply will directly relate to where you are at in your career—at the top of the ladder as a seasoned executive, say, or at the beginning of your journey as a new professional—along with the particular circumstances you find yourself in.

You will notice that Part 1, "You First," is devoted to the relationship you have with yourself. This is one area that may take the most courage and truth telling on your part. My belief is that a great beginning, with time spent on the foundational, introspection work advocated for in Part 1, will allow you to get the most out of the ideas in the Boss, Peers, and Team sections when it comes to applying them.

The good news, however, is that you can start anywhere in *The Courage Solution* that feels best for you. You may naturally gravitate toward the "Lead Your Boss" section if you are looking for ways to improve that relationship. Conversely, you might be needing a boost in how you engage and inspire those you lead, or want to transform your relationships with your peers. *Go where you have the greatest need right now, because the minute you start courageously engaging in a new and different way, you will begin to experience the positive benefits.*

No matter the scenario, my wish is for you to have greater fulfillment in your professional life *in the most efficient and effective way possible. The Courage Solution* isn't the end-all-be-all book on business leadership and career management. I don't know if that is even possible. It is simply a collection of simple and practical, but supremely powerful, methods that when applied courageously and wisely can make all the difference.

PART
1

You First

ABOUT
"YOU FIRST"

PART 1, "YOU First," is foundational to transforming your professional life for the better. All four parts of this book focus on things you can do to shift your experience. The other three parts begin with the premise that there are straight-forward, actionable things you can do to begin to have a more meaningful impact on all the people you encounter—your boss, peers, and colleagues, and your direct reports. My recommendations are based on the principle that *you are creating the reality you are experiencing.* The relationship you have with yourself is primary, because how you view the world flows from how you see yourself and what your philosophy is on how the ol' universe works.

From the statistics presented in the media today, it would seem that most professionals have a fairly dim view of the world, their professional lives, and the companies at which they work. Undoubtedly, that can be discouraging to them. But it's okay; there is hope—even if those stats generally reflect how you are feeling right now.

This section is about getting you in tune with yourself and exposed to helpful ways to stay on track so that you come from a place of power (forgive me here, but I am going to use the "a" word)—your *authentic* self—as opposed to coming from a place of fear. Or anger. Or ennui.

In order for you to effectively lead others—whether those in authority over you, around you, or working for you—you must be able to lead and manage yourself first. And that will require loads of courage and truth telling.

Here's a preview of what you'll find in Part 1:

Chapters 1 and 2 cover the importance of self-knowledge and self-awareness to creating a fulfilling life.

Chapter 3 lays out why it is imperative that you have your own personal "pit crew," and how to get one.

Chapter 4 shares a simple but incredibly powerful monthly technique that will help you stay in tune with all aspects of your life.

Chapter 5 provides practical, time-tested approaches to managing the daily madness of your professional life.

Chapters 6, 7, and 8 focus on how to help you successfully manage your career and increase your likelihood of advancement.

Chapter 9 is a mini chapter on how to be a great mentee.

And Chapter 10 tells you step by step how you can take a worry-free unplugged vacation.

Chapter 11 pulls it all together in a concise recap.

Magic begins to happen in your life when you embrace the truth that the only thing you can change is yourself. And I assure you that there are tangible steps you can take to get in the driver's seat of your professional life, giving you increased fulfillment, a greater sense of purpose, and more joy and energy every day.

Let's get started!

1

To Know Yourself Is to Love Yourself...
Just Not *Too* Much

'LL NEVER FORGET reading the results from the first 360-degree survey of my career.*

I was shocked! And angry. And hurt. And, and, and... I couldn't even think straight I was so upset!

Did my direct reports *really* think I was too tough on them?

Did my peers *really* think I moved too fast and didn't bring people along?

Did my boss *really* think I didn't think enough before taking action?

Yes. Yes, they did.

I resolved at that moment that I was *never* going back to work *again* if this is what these people thought of me! They made me sound like I was an intense, workaholic, overachieving, ambitious wrecking ball of a human being.

---

* A 360-degree survey is a questionnaire given to the boss, peers, and direct reports of the leader being evaluated. The leader themselves also completes a self-assessment on the same leadership traits. The results are aggregated anonymously by subgroup, and a report is supplied to the leader.

Ahem.

Well... uh... yes. That ended up being true too. But that wasn't *all* they said about me. There were some good things—some very good things—but I couldn't see it, or absorb any of that feedback, because I was so fixated on my deficits.

And magnifying the constructive feedback into epic proportions so much so that I wound myself right up into a defensive, close-minded ball and vowed NEVER. TO. TAKE. ANOTHER. 360. SURVEY. AGAIN.

Do you see how my tendencies for being tough (on myself most of all, by the way) and acting without thinking, along with my general intensity, might have influenced how I reacted to the feedback?

In retrospect, the way I reacted is humorous and somewhat embarrassing because now it is so clear that I undervalued the positive feedback and overemphasized the constructive. But in that moment, I was devastated and finding it very difficult to have any perspective whatsoever.

This is generally what happens any time we are faced with the truth about ourselves. It is shocking and uncomfortable. It brings up every deep-seated insecurity we have about ourselves.

Fortunately, part of my process of responding to the survey results was to have an excellent external coach walk me through the feedback (hold my hand, dry my tears—*whatever*) and support me in putting the messages (*all* the messages) into perspective so that I could identify one or two traits that needed improving.

Fast-forward 15 years, to when I sat with a brilliant organization psychologist as he walked me through my most recent 360 results, which were about to be shared with Jim Beam's board of directors. There were still OMG?!? moments, but overall I felt that the messages were exactly on point—my areas of strength were clear and my gaps were equally clear—and none of it was a surprise to me.

This time I didn't go into internal histrionics or go home and eat a loaf of warm, crusty bread with a hunk of gooey Brie cheese and wash it all down with a lovely pinot noir (well, I *might* have... but it wasn't because of my survey results).

What made the difference?

I was still an imperfect human being, leading imperfectly—so there was plenty of feedback to go around. What had changed?

Me.

I had changed. Because for many, many years (since that first emotionally exhausting process), I had systematically been working on growing my self-awareness so that I could change, grow, and manage myself better.

To begin to acknowledge and accept that who I was, what I believed, and how I was impacting those around me through my behavior was creating the reality I was living.

And that the only thing I could reliably change or control was me.

At the same time that I was going through this in my professional life over those many years, I was learning this in my personal life as well. At one critical point, I was navigating the aftermath of a divorce, healing from a very difficult marriage, and learning how to be a single mother to a toddler while the father of my baby was MIA.

On a daily basis, I was forced to look in the mirror of my life and acknowledge that I had made the choices that landed me where I found myself. And that if I wanted something different, I had to be different myself. I had to *choose* differently.

Now, this may seem an unpleasant approach for many of you reading this. Because it is far more comfortable to blame others for where you find yourself. For instance:

I could have spent a lot of time being angry at my ex—why couldn't he have been a better husband?

I could have spent a lot of time being angry at my parents—why couldn't they have been normal and given me and my siblings a happy, safe childhood?

I could have spent a lot of time being angry at the universe—why does everyone else have it so easy?

The same for work . . . and that first 360-degree survey report.

I could have spent a lot of time being angry at my direct reports—didn't they know how hard I work and how much I expect of myself?

I could have spent a lot of time being angry at my peers—why didn't they reach out to me if they wanted to understand where we were heading? In other words, I shouldn't always have to bring them and their team along.

I could have spent a lot of time being angry at my boss—just because he is slow to make decisions and take action doesn't mean I have to be that way!

And I did spend my fair share of time feeling and thinking all of these things. (What can I say? I'm a work in progress.) But ultimately, my personal and professional life would have been filled with more of the same if I had chosen to stay angry or feel victimized rather than take accountability and begin to change. To change myself so that I could have a different, more positive impact on those around me, and a much happier, fulfilling life.

So what about you?

How well do you really know yourself?

How self-aware are you?

Did you get really angry and defensive the last time you received 360-survey feedback? That's natural ... at first. But what did you do about it? (If you've never received a 360, go ask for one now—it *will* make you better!)

Marshall Goldsmith is the author of one of my favorite books, *What Got You Here Won't Get You There*. I especially like the section titled "Twenty Habits That Hold You Back from the Top." Goldsmith highlights many self-defeating traits that, for some seemingly mysterious reason, are so difficult to recognize in ourselves—yet we don't have any trouble seeing them in other people. Please go grab his book and read it. It's a quick read (it even has an accompanying workbook) and can help you look in the proverbial mirror and increase your self-awareness.

In the four parts of this book, I talk a lot about the value of courage, of being bold (wisely) and telling the truth to your colleagues (again, wisely). But this will ring hollow if you do not do the same with yourself.

Getting real with yourself about who you really are, what you are fabulous at (both naturally and learned), and what your icky tendencies are when you are stressed and not at your best is essential to having greater personal fulfillment and professional success.

Transformation starts with you.

Being real with yourself and getting clear is an incredibly important foundation for every other aspect of leading your life.

If you don't know who you really are (and are too afraid to ask your loved ones and coworkers), there are a few books I highly recommend you read (see page 242).

A LITTLE GENDER side dish for you to nosh on:

Guys—my observation of your tendency when it comes to self-awareness is to be overconfident and dismissive of any and all critical feedback. If you are going to lean in a direction, it tends to be toward self-satisfaction, not self-discovery. Watch out for that.

> Being bold and telling the truth to your colleagues will ring hollow if you do not do the same with yourself.

Gals—you have the opposite tendency from the guys. Your first natural response is to assume *all* feedback about you is correct, and you have a laundry list of things to improve upon before you can ever advance in your career (i.e., you believe you must be perfect to progress).

Neither approach is useful. Guys, you would benefit from some of the gals' humility—and gals, you would benefit from some of the guys' bravado.

Just sayin'.

2

The Personal Declaration

IN THE PREVIOUS chapter, I spoke about getting to know yourself, taking ownership of your life, and being accountable for the impact you are having on those around you. I also urged you to avoid falling hopelessly in love with your own fine self as it is right now or—conversely—being overly critical and striving for perfection. The outcome of all this self-knowledge is expressed in a Personal Declaration.

I first encountered the concept of a Personal Declaration while working at Campbell Soup Company, when Doug Conant was the CEO.* He taught me the importance of speaking from the heart in important relationships at work, and called it declaring yourself.

---

* Former CEO of Campbell Soup Company; coauthor with Mette Norgaard of *TouchPoints: Creating Powerful Leadership Connections in the Smallest Moments*; founder and CEO of ConantLeadership; chairman of the Kellogg Executive Leadership Institute at Northwestern University. In addition to holding all these fancy titles, Doug is simply a wonderful, wise human being.

The essence of declaring yourself is telling people who you are, what you think, and what you feel about work, life, leadership, and whatever else is important to you. This idea resonated with me and evolved into the Personal Declaration process that has been my practice ever since.

Over time, a Personal Declaration can be brief and straightforward or more fully developed, but the first step is capturing what makes you tick in a simple one-pager. You will see in Part 2, "Lead Your Boss," and in Part 4, "Lead Your Team," the very practical and beneficial utility of this practice. So go ahead and fill this in.

PERSONAL DECLARATION WORKSHEET

AREA TO SHARE	PERSONAL DETAILS
Family I come from (where I was born and raised; number of siblings)	
Family I'm part of now	
What's important to me outside of work (my passions)—list no more than five	
My motto or life philosophy (in a sentence— this is not a monologue)	
My values	
My greatest strengths (what I am naturally good at) professionally	
What I'm lousy at (things I dislike to do at work)	
The one thing I'd do in life if money were no object	

It can be surprisingly time-consuming to distill your views on life into succinct answers to these questions. Brevity is the challenge. Clarity is the very worthwhile reward.

This is not a one-time exercise. You can revisit it and evolve your answers as you evolve as a leader and as a human being.

TWO SAMPLE PERSONAL DECLARATIONS

TO GIVE YOU a sense of what the completed Personal Declaration worksheet may look like, I asked two executives to share their own Personal Declarations. Both are longtime friends and former colleagues, so I can attest to their authenticity.

> It can be surprisingly time-consuming to distill your views on life. Brevity is the challenge. Clarity is the very worthwhile reward.

The first example is from a colleague who has been using this tool for many years to hold himself accountable, along with having one-year, five-year, and lifetime personal and professional goals (the latter he calls the "special sauce"). Here is what his looks like.

SAMPLE PERSONAL DECLARATION WORKSHEET #1

AREA TO SHARE	PERSONAL DETAILS
Family I come from (where I was born and raised; number of siblings)	• Buffalo, NY • Irish Catholic • Family of six
Family I'm part of now	• Wife—Betty Sue • Four children, one adopted, ages 15 to 24
My passions (what's important to me outside of work)	• Family • Friends • Health and fitness (compete in minimum of two races/triathlons per year) • Coaching and mentoring kids (mine and others)
My guiding principles	• Carpe diem! • If you live your life free of failure, you're not taking enough risks • Live life with a fire that is *never* extinguished • To change is to grow • There is no such word as "can't"
My defining traits	Passion, optimism, positive energy, candor, authenticity, giving, grit
My development areas	• Speed to decision making (move too fast at times) • Overly blunt • Can come across as insensitive
Personal goals	Live in a perpetual state of learning, development, and fitness . . . of the mind and body
Professional goals	Be recognized as a leader and change agent who delivers exceptional results through innovation and risk taking

The second example comes from a highly successful executive who has only in the past few years adopted the practice of a Personal Declaration. A new hire shared her declaration with him when she joined the company, and this leader immediately recognized a good idea and adopted it for himself. Below you'll see how he articulates his declaration, which he calls a "join up."

SAMPLE PERSONAL DECLARATION WORKSHEET #2

PRIORITIES
Family—divorced/three kids. One in college; two in high school.
Career—get business growing globally and drive significant improvement across all of our brands globally. Build a more self-sufficient, talented marketing organization.
Personal enrichment—beach, reading, fishing, traveling to warm places in the winter, NFL football, LA Lakers
Health—golf, ski, run, gym. I'm a healthy "fat guy"... constantly fighting the pounds. *Kryptonite*: jelly beans and pizza.

STRENGTHS	WEAKNESSES
• Build highly collaborative relationships to get things done • Have good marketing skills combined with strong GM/business approach. I understand how markets work. • Empower teams to get their work done • Enjoy removing obstacles for people and acting as a "shock absorber" to drama above when I can • Self-deprecating, quick sense of humor that I use strategically to diffuse drama, confront people on issues or lighten a situation	• Tendency to avoid conflict. I don't like "extreme" points of view on either side and avoid them. • When pressure strikes, I will take work on myself vs. communicate and delegate • Poor at organizing and prefer more spontaneous things (i.e., great at "stop by and chat"; poor at well-organized meetings) **Blind Spots** • I tend to give people the benefit of the doubt too often • Don't say "no" enough • Not making people feel like they are appreciated enough (although I do appreciate them)

PREFERRED COMMUNICATION STYLE

- Verbal for complicated issues and matters of strategy
- Written for action, follow-up, and execution (and for simple questions)
- Tend to be casual at first and casual always

WHAT I VALUE MOST	WHAT I VALUE LEAST
- People with a sense of humor and empathy for their team and people - People who can simplify the most complicated issues down to an essence (i.e., short deck) - Big ideas that stretch us and challenge us (and finding a way through it) - Process that avoids problems in the future, but not process for process sake - Marketers who are culturally connected (digital, social, pop culture, fashion, movies, television, music) whether they like it or not. Intellectually curious. - Knowing your business. What are the five numbers that are most important *right now* to know? - Leaders who don't need to be prompted and are self-directed to take the reins	- Drama - Lack of vision (tactics all the time) - Nonenterprise-wide thinking - Power-hungry people - Complicators - Really needy people

BRIEF EDUCATION/WORK HISTORY

- Born and raised in Florida
- Undergrad at Texas Tech
- MBA at Harvard
- Worked for three companies my whole career

OTHER

I am an INTJ in MBTI and I am an introvert. While it may surprise you, I get energy from being alone, not from others. Walking into a big room of people that I have to say hello to, talk to, etc., is work for me. (Although I don't mind doing it, it's still work.)

I will not be the last one at the bar. For two reasons: (1) I value sleep and if I don't get six hours, I am shit. (2) Nothing good (from a work perspective) happens after midnight, so rather than put myself or my team in a weird situation, I vaporize.

As you can see from these samples, both executives have tweaked the Personal Declaration to reflect how they approach life and business, along with their preferred degree of openness in sharing with others.

There is no one right or best way to approach this—the key is just to do it. You will use the information you've captured here when you read Chapter 12 in Part 2, "Lead Your Boss," and Chapter 27 in Part 4, "Lead Your Team."

3

Why You Need a Personal Pit Crew

HAVE YOU EVER felt isolated and alone as you've navigated various professional and personal challenges?

I know so many mid-level business professionals who think that you climb to the top of the ladder by being some sort of individual corporate warrior. Yet all of the successful business executives I've worked with are open about the fact that they have a small group of trusted advisors who help them navigate their professional and personal lives.

When Doug Conant became CEO of Campbell Soup Company, he quickly gathered his group of advisors to spend a few days with him, to provide their perspective on the company and how he should go about leading it. That's a good example of using your pit crew for support in a massive professional transition (although I'm quite certain Doug doesn't call his posse his "pit crew").

A pit crew is a group of people who help a racecar driver stay on the track during a race, going as fast as possible for as long as possible. Racecar driving is a team sport. You can have the best driver and the best car, but without that pit crew, you aren't going to win.

It's the same with winning in business. It's a team sport. But not in the traditional way people talk about collaboration and teamwork in the workplace. That's important. But in order for you, as an individual, to be as fulfilled and successful as you desire, you need a team of people who support you.

Having a pit crew is *personal,* and support can take many forms. Some members of your pit crew will help you navigate your career. Others will help you navigate your daily life.

> **Some members of your pit crew will help you navigate your career. Others will help you navigate your daily life.**

An executive I know has moved his family of six several times to various parts of the world. When he was facing yet another move, he reached out to his longtime financial advisor, his best friend, and his former colleagues to get their perspective—not just about the impact of the decision on his career but also its impact on his wife and children, and on the overall fulfillment of their lives.

It's important to be selective about your pit crew. Mine includes a half dozen people—most of whom have known me for years or even decades—whom I can ask for advice, vent to, or share both good news and bad. They understand how I'm wired, love me in spite of myself, and know the world of business, so they "get it" without my having to explain a whole lot.

I also have a few people who provide practical, day-in-day-out support so that my life runs as efficiently and effectively as possible. As a single mom of a 13-year-old boy, who raised him while also climbing the corporate ladder, I can speak to how important it is to have a pit crew providing both professional and practical life support.

Sometimes I have a good handle on all the pressures, stressors, and demands in my life. But often I simply lose the plot and need someone to help me get perspective back.

Life is going to happen to you. You will change jobs, change companies, change industries. You may change cities. Or countries. Or continents. You may marry. You may divorce. You may raise kids. Or dogs. Or plants. You will have good bosses and bad bosses, good teams and bad teams. Your company will win some. And lose some.

Life will happen. Going it alone is a bad strategy. Never letting your guard down to people you can trust is a recipe for disaster. You need an external group of people committed to your success in your work and in your life.

But how do you build a pit crew if you don't already have one?

STEP 1: HAVE THE RIGHT MINDSET

BE WILLING TO be vulnerable. To admit when you are confused. Scared. Unsure. Dr. Brené Brown, research professor, licensed social worker, and author of multiple *New York Times* Best Sellers, has spent her entire career studying vulnerability. She defines it as the "willingness to show up and be seen with no guarantee of outcome."

Be willing to ask for help. Know that you need it, that you don't have all the answers—and won't—which is okay. That's normal. And human.

Executives, no matter how senior they are, are definitely *human*. You're surely aware of that when you're in the mid-level of an organization, looking up at all the fallible human beings running your company.

You're human too. And guess what? The people below you are thinking the same thing about *you* that you are thinking about your bosses.

STEP 2: IDENTIFY PEOPLE YOU TRUST

THINK ABOUT THE people in your life whom you really, really trust.

Is there anyone who has known you a long time—perhaps a supplier partner whom you have worked with at several companies? How about an executive coach? Is there a consultant whom you really value not only for their intellectual gifts but for their character as well? What about a former peer who keeps confidences and gives you great advice? Do you have a former boss or board member who really likes you and whom you respect and admire?

> In business, success at a high level is very difficult to sustain when you lack support in every area of your life.

Your pit crew will consist of people who can help you in some essential manner in your overall health and well-being, not just in your professional advancement. Because in business, success at a high level is very difficult to sustain when you lack support in every area of your life.

My mentor is in my pit crew. She is someone I absolutely revere, and her professional credentials are extraordinary and inspiring. But more importantly, she is a role model for me in my personal life as well. When we talk, her wisdom and perspective cover everything I might need to know from her. Sometimes we talk about company strategy. Sometimes about how my romantic partner and I are doing. Sometimes about spiritual topics. She's funny. She's brilliant. She's wise. And she calls me on my crazy. I'm lucky to have her and I know it.

Another member of my pit crew has known me for well over a decade. I know precisely how long he has been an incredibly important part of my life. We met when I was pregnant. I was working 16 hours a day and determined to do everything perfectly. His kindness, business perspective, and admonitions to take care of myself were game-changing for me. Over the years, our respect for each other's capabilities has enabled us to provide support and insight about each other and the companies we worked for at critical junctures. We've even partnered in business from time to time. Priceless.

Your pit crew probably should not include friends from work. Those are colleagues. They're important, but they are also swimming in the same water you are. Their viewpoint is important, but it may not be distant enough from the day-to-day grind to help shift your own perspective when you most need it.

STEP 3: INVEST THE TIME

YOUR PIT CREW surrounds you with loving support, practical advice, and fresh perspective. Your pit crew provides you with the fuel to do your best. But they can't do that if you don't stay in regular contact with these very important people whom you respect and trust.

To ensure that your pit crew is there when you most need it, you must be conscious about cultivating those relationships over time. With intent.

I speak only three or four times a year to some members of my pit crew. I talk with others on a monthly or weekly basis. But it's not only when "something is up." The constant is consistent connection.

Gratitude is also ever present. The members of my pit crew know how important they are to me and my ongoing success because I often remind them of that. I know down to the depth of my being that I simply would never have made it alone—that I could not have achieved what I have in my life without their support. Not possible. Period.

Just as members of your pit crew are there for you, you need to be there for them. It's a reciprocal relationship.

So tell the members of your pit crew how they help you, and why you value their counsel and advice. Say thank you. And just as they are there for you, you need to be there for them. It's a reciprocal relationship. My pit crew knows I am there for them anytime they need me.

MAKING IT IN business and in life is tricky, lonely, challenging, frustrating, disheartening, and discouraging at times. But you don't have to go it alone. And, in fact, if you try to be an individual corporate warrior you are unlikely to succeed or achieve as much as you could if you only let your guard down and seek out the help of people who love you and whom you trust, admire, and respect.

List your pit crew here:

- _____

- _____

- _____

- _____

- _____

4

Monthly "Weigh-Ins"—
The Transformational Power
of the Life Scale

N TODAY'S BUSINESS environment, the separation between our personal and professional lives is breaking down. There is growing acknowledgment that great leadership is akin to living a great life: it goes far beyond achievement and amassing the traditional trappings of success. It is also about being healthy, feeling fulfilled, being more purpose-driven, and making time for fun, family, and friends. I firmly believe that as you become more fulfilled in your life overall, you'll be better able to fulfill your professional responsibilities.

> Great leadership is akin to living a great life. It is about being healthy, feeling fulfilled, being more purpose-driven, and making time for fun, family, and friends.

Northwestern University's Kellogg School of Management has brought on the personal development author Deepak Chopra as adjunct professor of executive programs. He emphasizes the need to be smart, to work hard, and to be spiritually fulfilled.

That might not be the way previous generations of corporate leaders saw things, but I believe it's a step in the right direction.

But what is an easy way to check in with yourself so you can manage your own total life fulfillment and consistently live up to the values and priorities you've articulated in your personal declaration?

I'll never forget how I was feeling a couple of weeks into my move to Sydney, Australia, with my then five-year-old son. My weekends were filled with visits to amazing beaches in picturesque towns, where we inhaled the salty smell of seawater, listened to the waves crashing in the surf, and ran around barefoot on the hot sand playing catch in the sunshine. We would eat fresh-caught fish and golden-fried chips, surrounded by happy, relaxed people talking in that awesome accent.

My weekdays were a tad different. Racing to get my son to his new school, driving white-knuckled on the "opposite" side of the road to the new office where I was the only female, the American, and from "Corporate" (that's the death trifecta right there). Juggling childcare and an intense travel schedule throughout Asia, trying to impress my new boss and new team, and generally trying to not be a big, fat failure given I was also the first single-parent executive in Campbell Soup's history that it had ever expatriated.

I was feeling a bit of performance pressure, to put it mildly.

So while I had my game face on (fake it 'til you make it, baby!), in retrospect, I don't know that I was handling it all as well as I thought I was.

A couple weeks after the big move, my new boss (who was terrific) mentioned casually that I might enjoy meeting this guy named Michael for a coffee. He said, "I meet him for a coffee every month. Just to talk. He's really smart. A little different. But he helps me work through things—gives me a different perspective. See what you think of him."

This recommendation, while understated, ended up being yet another game-changer for me. Since I met this business wizard, he has been a core member of my personal pit crew (see the previous chapter) and someone whom I have had a literal or virtual coffee with almost every month for over eight years now and counting.

In our first conversation, the brilliant Michael Hall, founder and CEO of business and leadership consultancy WildWorks, based in Sydney, introduced me to an utterly simple but amazingly powerful tool that helped me get a handle on my complicated and overwhelming circumstances. And over time, I've adapted it to what I am going to share with you here, because it has helped me time and again to find my center, no matter my circumstances. It's a tool that helps me grow every time I use it.

Best of all? It's a terrific way to manage your life fulfillment and it takes very little time each month. I call it the Life Scale.

THE LIFE SCALE

HEART	MIND
BODY	SPIRIT

Just as stepping on a bathroom scale will give you an immediate picture of what is happening with your body weight, this Life Scale tool will provide you with an immediate snapshot of what is happening in your life.

Unlike a regular scale—which many health experts advise weighing yourself on daily or weekly—the Life Scale is a monthly check-in. And it doesn't take long. In fact, stepping on the Life Scale can take as little as three minutes each month. Here's the definition for each quadrant in the image above:

- The **Heart** quadrant captures all the people and activities and relationships in your life that fill up your heart. This is where friends, family, lovers, and romantic partners all reside. This area captures the activities and endeavors that make you feel loved and where you give love.

- The **Mind** quadrant captures all the people and activities that drive your professional fulfillment. Your job falls in this quadrant, plus all your relationships at work, whether with your boss, peers, team, or customers. This area also captures activities that drive your intellectual and mental stimulation and fulfillment.

- The **Body** quadrant is all about your health and well-being. It is about the activities and habits that nourish you and provide you with the energy and vitality you need to be at your peak. It's the fuel you ingest (oh, how I wish steak, bread, chocolate, and cheese were nutritional requirements!) and the movement and rest you give yourself.

- The **Spirit** quadrant houses the people, activities, communities, and habits in your life that fill and support your soul.

They can encompass religious or spiritual practices, community or group participation, service projects, time in nature, meditation, or mindfulness.

You may be thinking, "Uh oh—this chick is getting way too airy-fairy for me. Deepak Chopra at Kellogg is one thing. But why should I care about this? I've got a big important job. I'm a serious professional. I want to advance. How can checking in with my heart, mind, body, and spirit help me get what I want?"

Through a poll of thousands of adults in the United States, researchers attempted to quantify Americans' levels of contentment and life satisfaction. Just 33 percent of respondents described themselves as "very happy."* That means that, statistically, only one of every three of you reading this are very happy in your life overall.

For those of you in the not-so-happy camp, do you think your mood might affect how you go to work every day?

The survey's authors also noted that, increasingly, Americans are recognizing the importance of living a fulfilling life, and taking steps toward doing so. So knowing *how* to pursue fulfillment, which is individualistic and will change over time, is key to your getting happier in your life. And thus more successful in your job. As well as making you a lot more fun to work with every day.

Knowing *how* to pursue fulfillment, which is individualistic and will change over time, is key to your getting happier in your life.

---

* Carolyn Gregoire, "Happiness Index: Only 1 in 3 Americans Are Very Happy, According to Harris Poll," *Huffington Post*, June 2013.

SO HOW DOES the Life Scale work? There are three simple steps to using it:

Step 1: *Capture what's working—what is making you happy.*

Step 2: *Identify what's not working—or what is missing.*

Step 3: *Pick one thing to do different/an area of focus for the coming month.*

My very first Heart-Mind-Body-Spirit check-in had all sorts of good stuff happening in the Mind quadrant (loved the new job) and Body quadrant (loved my new active lifestyle), but besides my son doing well, my Heart and Spirit quadrants were both pretty empty of relationships and activities. I was lonely. I had no friends. No affiliations outside work. So I decided to focus on making friends—the Heart quadrant (I'd address the Spirit quadrant later).

THE THREE-MINUTE CHALLENGE

NOW IT'S YOUR turn to get on the Life Scale and see for yourself. I'm going to demonstrate how easy it is for you to do this each month.

In the space below (or on a separate sheet of paper if you can't stand the idea of writing in this hallowed book), capture what is working in your life in all four quadrants. Spend only 30 to 60 seconds on this. Then take another 30 to 60 seconds to capture what's missing or not working in all four quadrants.

HEART	MIND

BODY	SPIRIT

Hmmm...what do you see?

Take a look at what you've written and then select *only one* of the four areas you want to focus on in the next month to grow your happiness and fulfillment. Then identify the *one thing* you are going to do to fuel yourself up.

Easy, right?

If you find yourself stuck about what to do for the quadrant you've selected, spend a bit more time by yourself and really get in touch with your gut feeling. If you draw a blank, ask a close friend for ideas. For inspiration, here are a few:

- Empty Heart quadrant? Schedule in some consistent time with your sweetheart (date night!) and stick with it. Or commit to being home for dinner with your family at least once a week.

- Perhaps the Mind quadrant is unfulfilled because you have a broken relationship at work that is getting in the way of both your fulfillment and impact. Prioritize addressing the conflict so you have more peace.

- If your gap is in the Body quadrant and you are low on energy, you might decide to get eight hours of sleep a night for the next month.

- Depleted in the Spirit quadrant? Maybe you've got out of the habit of having your daily quiet time by walking the dogs. Reinstate that daily walk.

CAN STEPPING ON the Life Scale a couple of minutes each month really help you *get centered and in tune with yourself*? Yes.

Can stepping on the Life Scale a couple of minutes each month really help you have a *greater sense of confidence about what you are doing right in your life*? Yes.

Can stepping on the Life Scale a couple of minutes each month really help you *bring yourself more joy and fulfillment*? Yes.

Using the Life Scale will affect your work life because anything that positively affects who you are—your heart, mind, body, and spirit—also affects the outcome of everything else in your life, including your performance on the job.

This tool is powerful because it gives you an *easy* way to get back in touch with your life—with what is working and what is out of whack. We can get so caught up in the busyness of our lives that we forget to look at ourselves in the mirror and take stock. Doing just that takes self-kindness, to value your own happiness and fulfillment enough to take the time, and courage, to tell yourself the truth.

But you can do it and it can be this easy.

Remember, this is about progress, not perfection (make that your mantra!). There has not been one time during all the years I have done this check-in when every area was perfect. That's not the point.

Life is messy.

Change is constant.

Stuff happens.

Imagine how much more powerful and in control you will feel by consciously moving in a direction to support your own fulfillment.

You are worth it.

5

Managing the Daily Madness

As I write this, I am using a new time/focus technique I came across in the last year (the Pomodoro Technique—more on this later). As a corporate executive junkie who is now an entrepreneur (code for "you're-on-your-own-good-luck-to-you-sucka!"), I am forever in search of the magic bullet that helps me work more efficiently. Doing so will enable me to devote more time to the people I love.

Work-life integration is clearly an ongoing battle. Countless stories in the media continue to relate that people are working harder, longer hours and rarely disconnecting from the technology tethering them to the job.

Overwork is an addiction. And it is rife in the corporate world. In the United States, it seems rooted in a solid foundation of puritanism that has oozed through our veins unabated over the centuries as we corporate warriors hack through our daily lives with a grim determinedness.

Didn't take a vacation last year? Good for you!

Never get off your mobile device—even on the rare occasion when you sit down with your family for dinner? Look how committed you are!

Feel frazzled, uncentered, a little paunchy, and sleep deprived? Well, that's just the price of winning the battle of office life!

What. Are. We. Doing. Here?

Legions of studies, researchers, and think tanks continue to churn out stats on why living like this is not only pleasureless but unhealthy.

A study published in *JAMA* suggests workplace stress may be as hazardous to health as smoking, high cholesterol, and other conventional risk factors for disease.* And the American Institute of Stress posits that job stress is the major stressor for most people and has escalated dramatically over the past decades.

Consultancies have sprung up solely devoted to helping the corporate tribe try to live (brace yourself—the "b" word is coming) a more balanced, effective, fulfilled life, with offerings like the Corporate Athlete course. Canyon Ranch has a special program for executive health. The Center for Creative Leadership has long advocated well-being for leaders in a program called Leadership at the Peak.

There has got to be a better way, people!

I experienced quite the rude awakening about myself when I moved from a big corporate job to what I do today (speaking,

---

* Ron Winslow, "Job Strain Can Be Risk Factor for Subsequent Heart Attacks," *Wall Street Journal*, October 2007.

writing, advising, teaching—all devoted to the corporate tribe I love). I expected to be transformed into a Yoda-like being that would quietly rise out of bed every morning; easily slip into my meditation practice; be an in-the-moment, happily engaged mother of my son; and work in productive chunks of time, leaving plenty left over for friends, family, and fun. What a fantasy!

After enjoying some time off the first summer following my transition, I tore into my new life the exact same way I had been living my daily life for the previous 20 years. Several months in, I realized that over the course of my career I had been blaming my employers for my "no life" life! But it simply wasn't true. I was now working for myself (best boss ever—ha ha!) and was exhausted, overworking, and not scheduling enough fun and recreation.

> We create our realities, and if we are stressed out, exhausted, and out of whack, that's not our boss's fault, or our company's fault, or our family's fault. It's our own.

Who was the common denominator in all of this? Me.

It was yet another reminder that we create our realities, and if we are stressed out, exhausted, and out of whack, that's not our boss's fault, or our company's fault, or our family's fault. It's our own.

We train others how to treat us. And it starts by how we choose to treat ourselves. Every day.

One of my brilliant mentors, who role models extraordinary success both in the corporate world (sits on big public-company boards, runs a company, has authored a book, has been a trailblazer her entire career) and in her personal life (she meditates daily, has raised three amazing children, is a loving wife, and enjoys deep friendships), reminds me again and again that *when you are the most stressed, that is when you need to slow down or stop and regain center and perspective.* But what we tend to do is exactly the opposite. We tend to push harder.

Why? I think part of it is that we are scared—scared that if we stop running so hard, we will actually have to contemplate the life we have built. Scared of failure. Scared of appearing weak. And scared that if we are not *achieving* or *accomplishing* something every minute of every day, we are somehow being lazy (my personal favorite).

But coming from a place of fear is never an abundance-driver in our lives.

Oh, I can hear you skeptics out there grumbling already!

"Mindy—fear has been the reason I've got to where I am in my career. It's been what has propelled me to the dizzying heights of success I now enjoy. It's healthy always being a bit scared."

Uh-huh.

But are you fulfilled? Do you have a sense of peace about how you are living your life? Beyond ego gratification (which I myself know is a delicious little treat), is your life filled with joy? At least most days?

One study of CEOs of public and private organizations found all of them expressing a significant degree of emptiness and dissatisfaction on a day-to-day basis, especially in light of all their years (decades!) of sacrifice to get to their role. It's a sobering but unsurprising finding.

What I've come to believe, and what I try to live in my daily life, is that true fulfillment lies in knowing both when and how to go hard *and* when to stop and refresh—and having the discipline to do it.

THE POMODORO TECHNIQUE

IN A SIMPLE but powerful way, this is where the Pomodoro Technique comes in.* Based on research showing that the human brain can sustain focus really well for about 25 minutes, the Pomodoro Technique organizes breaks of 5 to 15 minutes at regular intervals, after which your whole system is primed to go back for another 25 minutes of focused, uninterrupted work.

I've discovered that using this technique is a huge driver of stamina (something super-important to us achievement junkies). If I follow the 25-5-25-5-25-15 pattern (I use my iPhone timer to keep track), I get a ton more done and have more energy at the end of the day. I know many professionals who are loving it too. It may be worth trying yourself.

There are other simple but powerful strategies and decision criteria that can help you get a handle on the daily madness.

ADDITIONAL HELPFUL STRATEGIES

HERE ARE THREE strategies that help me when I get overwhelmed or off-track:

1. *"Learn to say 'no' to the good so you can say 'yes' to the best."* I love this quote from personal development author John C. Maxwell. It's a mantra that has saved me again and again, and has helped me decline interesting, good but time-sucking opportunities in order to have space in my life for activities, people, and responsibilities that are aligned with my values.

---

* See www.pomodorotechnique.com.

2. *Stephen R. Covey's urgent/important four-box model as an aid in prioritizing your endless to-do list.* We tend to think that the urgent stuff cropping up every day is what we should be addressing. As a result, we don't focus on the valuable, important work we are actually hired to do. Go reread Habit 3, Put first things first, in *The 7 Habits of Highly Effective People*, for a refresher on this super-useful tool. There are many great videos online showing Covey proving his point about prioritizing wisely by having someone struggle with some rocks and sand.

3. *Planning ahead.* The night before. The week before. The month before. It's not sexy, people, but it works. You will experience a notable reduction in your stress level when you take a few moments each evening to peruse your schedule for the following day, note the one to three important items that have to be done (and that will make you feel great for having accomplished), and calendar them in. Same principle at the end of each week. And month. It's a game-changer. Trust me.

I read a terrific article in *Harvard Business Review* by Ed Batista entitled "The Most Productive People Know Who to Ignore." As an executive, you have to get comfortable with the fact that someone will always be disappointed because they didn't get the amount of your time that they wanted—so you have to prioritize who that will be. This struck a chord as I reflected on my life at Jim Beam, where I constantly had people lined up outside my office door and back-to-back meetings, rarely took lunch, and always felt guilty that there weren't enough hours in the day. And this was before I even contemplated my responsibilities as a single mother.

I had to accept that it wasn't possible to give everyone everything they needed. My job was to be selective and understand that some people would always be disappointed (which wasn't the end of the world). Accepting this was quite liberating—and something I wish I had understood much earlier in my work life.

I loved hearing about Stephen Sondheim's practice of composing for 20 minutes and then napping for 10 from my son's band teacher.* He was emphasizing the need for us parents to allow our kids to have plenty of breaks from practicing—they would perform better as a result. I immediately thought of all of us in the corporate tribe and that we should be so wise.

Endless resources are available to help you gain more control over your daily experience. I've shared a few of the tools and strategies that help me. The bigger point here, though, is that you have to decide that living a more fulfilled life on a daily basis is a priority for you.

> **You have to decide that living a more fulfilled life on a daily basis is a priority for you.**

You have to decide that you are worth treating with more respect.

You have to be willing to get off the high of adrenaline and ego so that you can be calmer, more centered, and more focused.

I haven't turned into Yoda . . . yet. But the days that I am more Yoda-like, I am happier, feel healthier, and have used my time more wisely.

---

* Stephen Sondheim, an American musical theater composer and lyricist, has received an Academy Award, eight Tony Awards, eight Grammy Awards, and a Pulitzer Prize, among other accolades. Clearly not a lazy man!

6

Why *Naming* It Matters in Career Management

S O FAR, WE'VE covered a lot of territory about how to drive your life fulfillment through courageous self-awareness; being focused on the heart, mind, body, and spirit areas of your life; and taking ownership of your daily experience (i.e., calm or chaotic). And you've been reminded that you are not alone, nor generally should you try to navigate your life and career in a solo fashion.

There is one area that does require solo attention, however. Your career aspirations.

I had a 10-year plan when I was 10 years old. A little weird, I know. I clearly saw that I wanted to go to college. And even at age 17, when I moved from Detroit, Michigan, to Pasadena, California, I knew I would go to graduate school. (Major nerd alert: I was *that* kid in elementary school, who thought it would be cool to read every book in the library... and very nearly did.)

This was probably more a result of a personality disorder than anything else, as neither of my parents had college degrees—both sides of the family were of Midwestern farm stock.

A decade later and I declare rather unashamedly that I want to be a chief human resources officer at a global company by age 40. I made this declaration to folks 15 years my senior who were all vying for the top job as well (clearly, not my most politically savvy moment).

I made it at age 39.

My point in sharing this is that there is an element in career management where you simply have to put it out there. Even if it is a bit bold and audacious (what some people call "boldacious"). (The big boss at the time of my declaration pulled me aside later for some coaching and told me that I shouldn't have been so self-centered. I was young and stupid enough to think she meant it when she asked all of us in a staff meeting where we wanted to go in our career.)

> **The first step to achieving anything great is being willing to name it.**

And then, of course, you work your tail off and stay open-minded about opportunities and build a track record of performance, and there is luck and timing, and all sorts of other factors.

For the sake of this chapter, I'm going to assume you have character and competence (both technical and leadership), so you're ready, willing, and able to put the time in to advance your career.

This is about *your* vision.

This is about *your* goals.

This is about where *you see yourself* in 1, 3, 5, and 10 years from now.

It's time to get a plan . . . and the first step to achieving anything great is being willing to name it.

NAME IT TO CLAIM IT

IN BUSINESS, AS in life, being clear about where you are headed is essential to getting there.

Companies spend countless hours and untold dollars figuring out their strategies and the plans to achieve those strategies.

What is astonishing to me, however, is the passivity many business professionals employ in their own careers. I have observed over and over the pregnant pause and verbal stutter after I ask a simple question such as "What would you like to be doing in five years?" Or "In what role do you see yourself in three to five years?"

> **Being clear about where you are headed is essential to getting there.**

Smart, capable, driven, and self-described ambitious business leaders have stared at me tentatively and then said things like, "I just want to be doing work I enjoy," or "I'd like to be making a difference," or "I'd like to maybe eventually be running X, Y, or Z. But not for a long time. I know it takes a lot to get there."

Many of these same nice, talented, hard-working folks are also the ones seeking development plans, career paths, and professional development programs from their employers. So while they don't know their own goals or ultimate aspirations (they can't *name it*), they sure want the company to have a P-L-A-N for them.

The problem with this approach is that the onus for career development and advancement is placed squarely on the company's broad, boxy shoulders (and deep pockets), with the implication that it is the company's job to figure it out.

But it's not. It's not the company's job to worry about your next career step. Or the one after that. It's your job. Honestly, why should it care more than you do? It has other obligations to meet:

- Your company has an obligation to deliver value to its shareholders.

- Your company has an obligation to pursue a longer-term strategy and put shorter-term plans in place to deliver that value.

- Your company has an obligation to make sure it has the right people with the right talents in the right roles at the right time to deliver that value.

"What?" you may be asking. "Doesn't my company have an obligation to develop *me*?"

Frankly, it has that obligation only to the degree that you are one of those people who have the talent and capabilities to deliver current and future shareholder value.

I know this may not sound very humanistic, but it's *your* job to know what you want in your life and career. Just like the company has an obligation to have a plan, so do you. For *your* career and your life.

Remember, the only thing you can reliably control at your company is yourself. And just like the company has to clearly articulate that longer-term plan, so do you.

Companies write it down, present it, and put their strategies on posters and in PowerPoint presentations. They do this for a reason: so that everyone is clear on where the organization is headed (and, hopefully, why). And within this clear framework, all decisions (resource allocations) are impacted by said strategy.

It provides clarity and focus, and it narrows choice. Which is actually quite freeing.

The company *names* it so it can *claim* it.

The same applies to you. You have to spend the time evaluating what matters to you, what you are passionate about, what you love to do, and where your greatest talents and weaknesses lie (see Chapter 2 for a refresher on this).

I won't bore you with too many stats, but your likelihood of getting what you want increases dramatically simply by clearly stating your goal—and especially by doing so in writing.*

Once you've contemplated what job you *really* would love to have, take a moment and fill in the following (it's okay to be bold, folks):

In _____ years I want to be in _____ role.

As time passes, your end goal may change—that's okay. Life is dynamic and we evolve as people. Our priorities change. But for now, it is important to be as clear as possible about where you are heading and why it's important to you.

I was driven to attain a role of global impact because I believed I had an obligation to lead and serve, and to be a

---

* In a 1979 study, students in Harvard's MBA program were asked, "Have you created clear, written goals for your future and made plans to accomplish them?" It turned out that only 3 percent had written goals, 13 percent had goals but not in writing, and 84 percent had no goals at all. Ten years later, follow-up interviews were conducted. The 13 percent of MBA students who had goals but had not written them down were earning twice that of the 84 percent who had no goals. And the 3 percent who had written goals had average earnings of ten times more than the other 97 percent of the class! Ashley Feinstein, "Why You Should Be Writing Down Your Goals," *Forbes*, April 2014.

positive force in a business. I had seen time and again the impact of poor leadership and I wanted mine to be the opposite of that. And to make a big, positive impact, I needed to be in a big job.

Not everyone has that ambition or vision for themselves. There is no right or wrong answer. The key is to be clear.

YOU KNOW THAT there is no shortcut to professional success. It requires hard work and talent. And to achieve sustained success, you also need character. You can have the greatest character and work ethic, and be super-talented, but if you are not clear where you are headed, you are less likely to get there than if you are.

Remember, you have to name it first to get on the path to claim it!

7

Ditch the Ladder, Embrace the Mosaic

N CHAPTER 6, we looked at the importance of clearly stating where you would like to end up by a certain time. Once you have done this, you are ready to be more strategic about your plan to get there.

So how do you plan and consider your choices once you are clear on where you want to end up?

One of the most helpful ways to think about career management is to see it as a mosaic, rather than as a ladder.

The best C-suite leaders I know have had a variety of both cross-functional roles and within-function depth, along with experience across multiple industries and/or geographies. Here's an example of a highly successful global CFO's career in mosaic form:

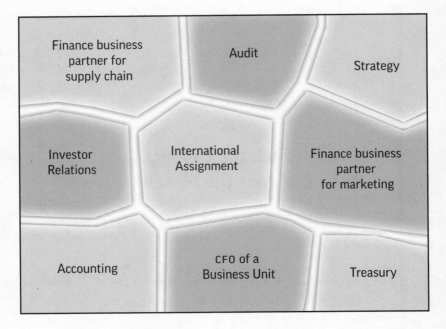

You'll note that that this executive worked in several functions (strategy, audit, and investor relations), not just pure, straight-up finance roles. He also said a big yes to an international assignment.

Because he viewed his career more laterally—and was willing to take lateral roles crossing functional boundaries—he was a far more effective, agile leader than he would otherwise have been. His diverse experiences were a huge factor in reaching the top job at a multibillion-dollar public company.

It is easy as you are building your career to get seduced into thinking that it is better for you to stay in one function, especially if you have a sponsor or big boss who likes you. The danger in this approach is that you limit your options down the road and don't build a more enterprise-wide mindset toward the business.

Take a moment now to consider in mosaic form your career choices thus far.

Now contemplate what options you could pursue in order to strengthen your candidacy for the dream job you identified in the previous chapter.

Use the blank career mosaic below to fill in the distinctive experiences, disciplines and assignments that demonstrate you have breadth not just depth.*

MY CAREER MOSAIC

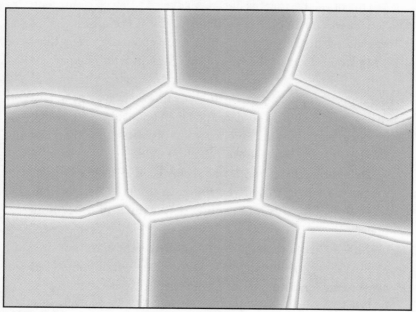

---

* There happens to be nine pieces in this blank mosaic. This is for illustration only. There is no ideal number.

You can then go have a conversation with your boss, mentor, or someone successful whom you admire and ask them to help you consider various next assignments and how those assignments support your end goal.

STAYING CONNECTED AND KNOWING YOUR WORTH

BUT WHAT IF you are considering a more significant change? Maybe either going to another company or, even more audaciously, starting your own?

One of the best pieces of career advice I received from Doug Conant was on an extremely stressful day at the office where I was aiding in the termination of two very senior executives. Doug stopped me in the hallway to check in after one particularly grueling conversation. After I had debriefed him on how the conversation had gone, he told me it was always a good idea to have my résumé up-to-date and my relationships with search firms current. He said, "You never know when you will be in a similar situation as these executives are today."

He went on to say how it was always good to *know your value* on the market so that if you did have to make a transition—whether voluntarily or involuntarily—you would be more prepared.

I have always remembered that advice and have not only applied it myself but shared it with others. When employees came to me for career advice, I would explicitly ask them if they had their résumés up-to-date and if they had relationships with the right people at the best search firms. Many employees would be initially shocked that I, as the head of HR, would advise this, but they quickly saw the wisdom in it (I was always sure to cite the Doug story). Some, however, would continually push off making the time to build relationships with recruiters and then be caught flat-footed and terrified when they needed those relationships the most.

You benefit immensely from keeping these relationships current, because these folks will naturally think of you when interesting opportunities arise, opportunities that may enhance your career mosaic. They will proactively seek you out, and you will have a chance to consider choices you may never have even dreamed possible.

And in the event that you are involuntarily terminated (no matter how good you are, it can happen), you will be able to easily connect with your network and clearly describe your ideal next role.

GOING SOLO

IT'S ESSENTIAL TO have long-term relationships with recruiters, and also with former colleagues, supplier partners, and associates at professional services firms you've worked with. These relationships are important even if you decide to start your own enterprise.

Choosing to go solo was an incredibly difficult decision for me. I was accustomed to the safety and security of the corporate environment. It was all I knew. But as I shared with you earlier in this book, I yearned to have a broader impact, and the only way that was possible was to take a leap of faith and start my own company.

> Make time to meaningfully expand your network. You'll benefit from hearing about the progress the people in your network are making in their work and life. And you'll get to share with them what you are navigating.

One successful entrepreneur expressed to me his surprise that more people haven't made the shift. He noted that after nine years of being self-employed, following a more traditional corporate career, he found it incredibly rewarding and wouldn't want to go back to his old life.

Having experienced both work models, I treasure the freedom and flexibility of the life I now lead. Yes, I miss being in a fast-paced environment working alongside super-smart people on a daily basis, and the camaraderie that brings. But I still rely on my network, as I did in the past. I have coffees with the same folks I did before. I call or email with the same frequency. And I carve out time to meet new people and have new conversations.

Remember one basic rule: The more people you know, the better. Because you never know who might think of you for a job opportunity or a consulting contract. "Out of sight, out of mind" is very real. So it's always worthwhile to stay in touch and keep those in your network informed of your professional activities. Similarly, make time to meaningfully expand your network. You'll benefit from hearing about the progress the people in your network are making in their work and life. And you'll get to share with them what you are navigating.

> **No matter how you choose to build out your career, thinking in terms of building both depth and breadth is essential.**

Most people are incredibly eager to be helpful and supportive. The only way you can give or receive that type of assistance is to make time for meeting with people. Although numerous social media platforms enable that, nothing beats an old-fashioned phone call or meeting for a cup of tea. You will never have "enough time." You just have to decide to make the time.

NO MATTER HOW you choose to build out your career, whether with in-company roles of various stripes or a blend of entrepreneurial and corporate endeavors, thinking in terms of building both depth and breadth is essential. That perspective will help you as you face career choices.

Remember that your career is a mosaic, not a ladder, and your best chance of building both depth and breadth in your career is to take roles outside your core function and geography. Roles that stretch you beyond your core functional expertise can not only bring you invaluable experience (I can honestly say that my appreciation for marketing, finance, and IT has skyrocketed since building my own company from the ground up) but can also provide a tremendous amount of satisfaction and personal confidence. And whatever path you choose to take, be sure to stay connected to others along the way.

8

Smarts Ain't Enough—You Gotta Have a Shtick!

NOW THAT YOU are clear on where you want to end up career-wise, it's time to talk about what you will look like on the way there. Form over substance... just this once, I promise.

Recently I spoke at a general counsels conference. Picture a sea of black suits, crisp white shirts, and sensible shoes. With the exception of a few snazzy pinstripes thrown in or a dash of charcoal gray, it was an undertaker's dream tribe. And this group included women!

I was there to speak on leadership to this über-smart, somber crew (or at least somberly attired), and I was appreciative when several attendees complimented me on the dress I was wearing.

But unsurprised.

Why? Because, unfortunately, it is still an anomaly to see a beautifully dressed woman in a corporate setting among a sea of suits. (I'm not saying *I'm* beautiful, I'm saying *the dress* I was wearing was beautiful.)

I'm a big fan of dresses. Of femininity. Of generally embracing the fact that, unless something has drastically changed overnight, I'm all woman. So it's helpful to dress that way... in an actual dress.

At work.

In the corporate world.

Surrounded by men.

But this chapter isn't just for the gals.

I've learned that how I present myself by what I wear and how I look makes a difference in the impact I make. That was instrumental to getting me into the C-suite and the boardroom. (Don't freak out here—there were also years and years of hard work, a track record of results, etcetera, etcetera, but we aren't talking about that in this chapter.)

This principle applies to the guys too.

While I'm all about substance over form, and every other chapter in this book is about substance, form matters too. A lot.

I learned this lesson—painfully, I might add—when I was working at Campbell Soup's HQ. But I'll get to that story in a moment.

IMAGE AND IMPACT

WE LIVE IN a society that's very impatient when it comes to making first impressions. People make snap decisions about other people. That might not be fair or right, but it's a fact.

How long do those snap decisions take? At the high end, 20 seconds, according to some studies. And often, that first impression doesn't significantly change after longer contact: when corporate hiring managers were shown 20-second videos of job applicants, their assessments remained unchanged even after they later spent 20 minutes with those same applicants.

But again, the 20-second figure is at the high end. Other studies suggest it takes just 7 seconds to form a first impression. And an article by two Princeton University researchers in the journal *Psychological Science* states that one-tenth of a second is all it takes to form a first impression that doesn't significantly change after longer contact.

Here's another painful reality: the more conventionally beautiful you are, the better you are treated. Right or wrong, a good-looking person is generally considered superior in intelligence, personality, and potential for success in comparison with a less-good-looking counterpart.

In one research study, subjects were shown photographs of people with average and above-average looks before engaging in phone conversations with them. Not only were expectations higher for the talks with attractive men and women, but those expectations were generally met—probably as self-fulfilling prophecies.

Studies show that women considered highly attractive have an 8 percent wage advantage over women of average looks, while women seen as below average in appearance pay a 4 percent wage penalty. Good-looking men gain a 4 percent wage advantage, with a 13 percent disadvantage for men seen as unattractive.

> **In order to have the positive impact on the job you desire, you gotta have a shtick.**

Shocking. Horrifying. Depressing. Enraging. Whichever adjective you choose to describe this situation, it's still true.

So in order to have the positive impact on the job you desire—in order for you to be taken more seriously (which means respected and listened to), and in order to get that promotion you believe should be yours—you gotta have a shtick.

And your shtick (both how you look and how you act) has to suit you and amplify your best attributes while also fitting in *just enough* so you don't scare the tribe you are a part of. (I say, keep 'em interested. Keep 'em guessing. But don't make them squirm, if you can help it.)

You need to know how to work what you got.

Yes, you bring the substance—you're smart and hard-working, you've got character—but you can help yourself and have even greater impact at work if you, dare I say it, dress for success.

I mentored a senior leader named Patrick who struggled mightily with this concept. He asked me to mentor him because he wanted to get promoted, and he just couldn't figure out why that wasn't happening for him. He had an excellent educational pedigree, multifunction experience, and a track record of successful delivery.

What was the problem? I knew Patrick. Knew the team he led. Knew his business results. And agreed that he had a ton of stuff in the plus column. But when it came to getting the BIG job, something was missing.

Part of it was the absence of a commanding air. He was just kind of beige.

I suggested that Patrick might see better results if he was more intentional about his leadership impact. That meant presenting himself with a bit more oomph. But he balked.

"I'm an introvert! I know I'm not that stylish, but I used to be in finance! And it shouldn't matter anyway!"

"Patrick, you are right. It shouldn't matter. But it does. And you are in marketing, my friend. Inspiring confidence and being a snappy dresser are part of the deal."

Patrick told me a week later that when he told his wife what I had said about transforming his "look"—about getting some *style* to go with all his substance—she heartily agreed. Apparently, she had been trying to get him out of his beige and khaki for many years but without success.

The combination of Patrick's innate quietness (which has a ton of benefits in the workplace as a leader) and his nondescript wardrobe added up to a lack of impact. Of gravitas. Of executive presence. Call it what you will.

People confer credibility according to the image you portray *and* what you say *and* what you know *and* what you do.

HOW I LEARNED MY LESSON

THERE I WAS, sitting rigidly in a chair across the large executive-style desk from a very senior leader, my palms sweating. I was trying not to cry in the office of the woman who had just said to me, "Mindy, it's time you started dressing more appropriately and looking like the senior leader you aspire to be."

As I stuttered and blubbered internally, she continued. "You have the smarts and potential, but you don't look the part. And if you don't look the part, you will never get there."

Here she paused dramatically and slowly perused my outfit with what seemed like disdain. My outfit was similar to what I had been wearing pretty much every day for the previous 12 months. Gray slacks. Maroon cable-knit sweater set. Chunky-heeled penny loafers. Clearly not winning any fashion contests, not even in Camden, New Jersey!

The only thing I was able to choke out was "I'm just waiting to buy new clothes once I lose the baby weight. I'll get new clothes then."

"Your son is three. He's not a baby. There are a lot of overweight executives. Don't wait to lose the weight to start dressing like an executive. Get an image consultant."

Boom.

I stood up stiffly, thanked her for her feedback (OMG?!?), and went home that night crying bitter self-pitying tears.

But once the tears dried, I really thought about what she had said. My wardrobe *was* awful. I *did* dress terribly (and felt terrible about myself). I knew she was right. I clearly needed help. And oh, by the way, I was working like a dog and wanted to get promoted badly. So I took her advice, even though I was in shock and my feelings were hurt.

I hired an image consultant, scraped together a budget for this turnaround project, and tried to keep an open mind. Here's what I learned:

Everyone needs a professional "uniform" that highlights their best features and minimizes their lumpy bits in order to project the most positive image.

Personal shoppers are the best! Not only are their services usually free, but they are devoted to helping you look your best. So to get help, you don't have to be loaded (I'm referring to money, not alcohol. Just sayin').

Everyone needs expert advice on grooming (women—that means hair *and* makeup; men—that means hair on your head, face, and, God forbid, neck) and a sustainable plan to continue with it on your own.

Let's break this down a bit.

The "uniform" is key. And a strategic investment. My consultant urged me to invest in a few high-quality pieces that would stand the test of time. They could be tailored if and when I lost weight, which I eventually did. Those pieces would be in optimal colors and fit for my body shape and skin tone. By wearing these core pieces—the uniform—with some creative accessorizing (think shoes, belts, jewelry, scarves), it would appear as if I had a much larger wardrobe.

The vital point here is quality over quantity.

And then there is the tailoring. Which is magical. Having things nipped and tucked so your clothes appear to have been molded to your body is transformative. Whether you're male or female, the single greatest relationship you can have is with an excellent tailor or seamstress who will alter *all* your clothes to fit your body. With expert tailoring, a simple shirt will look like a designer piece.

Every major department store has personal shoppers on staff. My advice is to go to a high-end department store and ask a manager to introduce you to a personal shopper, who will help you, a busy business professional, with your wardrobe needs. Mention that you don't have a huge budget at the moment. You want someone who wants to build a long-term relationship and will help you look your best on your modest means.

Be honest! This will serve you well, because you do not want to be hooked up with someone who pushes items on you. You want someone who will get to know what suits you best and will notify you of sales and new arrivals.

High-end department stores also employ genius tailors; often, you can get the items you purchase there altered for free or at a nominal cost.

DAZZLE WITH YOUR WOMANLINESS

For all you female investment bankers, lawyers, consultants, and business executives out there who are still mad at me for my embrace-your-femininity-and-wear-a-dress comment at the beginning of the chapter, here's something to consider: if a man is a misogynist, he's not going to respect you any more by dressing like him or being dowdy. Dazzle him with your womanliness. You're already smarter than him anyway.

Or you can bypass this in-person process and use an online personal stylist company that caters to busy professionals who want to dress better. As a subscriber, you'll fill out a profile that includes details about budget, body measurements, and your desired look—whether it be casual, business, or more formal.

You stipulate the items of clothing you want and—voilà—a box arrives at your home containing clothing for you to try on and select from. You send back whatever you don't want, keep the rest, and you're on your way. This is a new business category that's definitely filling a need and is sure to grow.

THE BOTTOM LINE

WHEN YOU ARE at your best, no matter your shape or size—in my case short and round and sturdy—damn my Scottish roots!—you'll have confidence. You'll project an air of command. You'll have that elusive thing called "presence."

When you combine that personal presence with your own brand of sassy—your shtick—and your hard work, smarts, and unique contributions, it's a mighty combination indeed.

9

Mentoring for the Mentee

"DOWN-TO-EARTH. PERSONABLE. BRUTALLY honest. Open about mistakes and lessons learned. Shared real help. Shared his network."

A good friend of mine, who happens to be a CEO, rattled off this list of attributes when I asked about her new mentor.

But why does a CEO have a mentor? She's not even a new CEO. Here are some reasons she *is* a CEO in the first place: she knows the power of learning from others and is humble enough to have a mentor as part of her personal pit crew.

There are dozens of books and resources and programs about mentoring. In my 20 years of leading HR, I've made the following observations about mentoring:

- Forced matches tend not to work; mentees have to *want* to be mentored by the person they are with.

- Many mentors talk about themselves aimlessly, rather than get to know their mentees and then target their stories and experiences.

- Many mentees are lazy and don't display any curiosity or real passion for learning—they don't come prepared to the discussions; they just want a sponsor for their next promotion.

- A lot of companies have their HR departments creating programs with lots of forms and process and check-ins, which generally annoy all parties (and the mentors don't adhere to the material anyway).

No matter your company or the program design, it is important to remember that the only thing you can reliably change or control is yourself. It is up to you as the mentee to maximize the experience you have in an informal or formal mentoring relationship.

And consider this: no matter how senior you are, you are never too old or too tenured or too high up on the corporate food chain to no longer benefit from a mentor. Learning doesn't stop until the body's in the box. So if you are without a mentor right now, it's the perfect time to seek one out.

ADVICE TO MENTEES

1. *You have the need—so show up and make it easy for your mentor to help you.* Mentors are busy. They mean well, and they likely have lots of wisdom to share, but if you don't manage the relationship effectively, you won't get what you need. Your mentor didn't ask for this time, you did. Always remember that. Be prepared. Take notes. Come with relevant questions. Be clear to your mentor about how he or she can help you. Don't waste time. You aren't entitled to this gift. So don't go to a mentoring meeting and, when asked what you want to talk about, reply, "I don't know."

2. *Don't argue when your mentor makes an observation about you.* Simply note it. Say "thank you." And consider later if you agree or disagree. You are there to receive, not debate feedback or perspective.

3. *Pay it forward.* When you've been in the enviable position of receiving mentoring, make sure you look for an opportunity to serve as a mentor yourself to someone. Start giving and sharing information to others early on. You will also quickly realize how annoying it is to have the desire to help someone who doesn't use *your* time wisely.

Receiving great mentoring from someone you admire and respect is a tremendous gift. Remember to return the favor.

Receiving great mentoring from someone you admire and respect is a tremendous gift. Remember to return the favor.

10

How to Take a Worry-Free Unplugged Vacation

SAVED THIS CHAPTER for the last in this section not because the topic isn't important but because it is. (I read somewhere that readers recall the last thing they read the most vividly.)

When I moved to Sydney from Camden, I'd never taken more than a one-week pseudo-vacation in my entire career. Then I land in this sunny place halfway around the world and watch people in the business I work in, from the CEO to my assistant, take three-week vacations without flinching.

What was going on?

The prevailing (judgmental) notion back at HQ, and an ongoing joke, was that getting an assignment in Australia was a vacation in itself. But it wasn't true. The people I worked with worked just as hard as their American counterparts and got just as much done. But they played much harder too—and had way more fun. Plus they actually took proper vacations where they unplugged from work and went off and had an amazing adventure with their family or friends. For weeks!

Fast-forward several years. I was reporting to the CEO of a multibillion-dollar company as chief human resources officer and nearing my first summer vacation. I reminded my boss and my colleague, the CFO, that I would be gone for two weeks (gasp!) and that I had deputized Tom, a direct report, to run things in my absence. I gave them the phone number of the hotel's front desk, letting them know that my mobile device would be turned off (put in the hotel room safe, no less, so I wouldn't be tempted) and I wouldn't be bringing my computer.

"If someone dies, give me a call. Otherwise I will see you both back here in two weeks" was my parting shot.

I didn't think twice about it ... in spite of the rather stunned and disbelieving looks I received.

When I walked back into the office Monday morning two weeks later, tanned, refreshed, and happy, the CFO pounced on me and exclaimed, "I can't believe it! You did it! We didn't believe you were serious about not being in contact. We sent you tons of emails and *you never responded*. You're crazy!"

"Did anybody die while I was gone?"

Nope.

"Did Tom mess anything up or make any crazy decisions in my absence?"

Nope.

"Are we still making and selling spirits?"

Yup.

"Well then, I guess we're okay."

After a 90-minute debrief with the CEO and CFO that morning, I was fully up-to-date, back in the swing of things, and life moved on as if I had never been gone. Perhaps the best part was that both the CEO and CFO later said to me privately that the fact that I had gone off on vacation and truly unplugged gave them hope that they could actually do it too.

It's pretty pathetic that, in today's day and age, disconnecting from work for a vacation—you know, that thing where you do no work?—is such a foreign concept, at least in the United States. Here is what I learned from my Aussie colleagues about ensuring it is a successful endeavor and one you will be able to repeat should you desire to try this yourself:

1. *You must deputize someone credible in your absence to cover your area and make decisions in your stead.* The more senior you are, the more important this is to do. Select a direct report with good judgment (though hopefully all of them have it, if you've hired well!) whom your peers and boss respect. Explain your rationale for your selection to your other direct reports and reinforce the expectation that they are to give their peer the same respect and responsiveness that they give to you. If you are an individual contributor, simply ask a coworker to cover your area of responsibilities in your absence and offer to do the same when they take a vacation. Make sure to clearly communicate this plan to your boss.

2. *Communicate broadly that this person is your proxy—and you must mean it.* State that you will honor all decisions made by this person and that this person should be treated as if he or she were you (this might actually be a curse rather than a benefit!).

3. *Reinforce that you will be completely unplugged.* While you are away, you will not be checking email, voicemail, or materials delivered by carrier pigeon. This is a great opportunity to walk your talk about your values and how important it is to be fully present with your family, your friends, or yourself, as it is essential to your overall well-being and is key to your

effectiveness on the job. (Most companies and executives pay lip service to these values but do not actively demonstrate it—now's your chance!)

Then it is time to actually walk out of the office, remove the needle from your arm (oops—I mean, turn your mobile device off), and go have some unfettered fun. Yes, fun. For, like, several days in a row.

I recall a group of high-powered executives gabbing about summer plans:

Smart dude #1: "Well, my boss usually goes on some exotic vacation and we never hear from him."

Me: "Is that what *you* do when you go on vacation?"

Smart dude #1 (boastfully): "No! I get on the laptop for three to four hours in the morning and then take the afternoon off. It's great! My boss loves it, and my family is used to it."

I no longer think smart dude #1 is very smart.

(And I am clearly enjoying my vacations more than he is.)

> **Walk your talk about your values and how important it is to be fully present with your family, your friends, or yourself.**

There is an underlying fear, arrogance, and bravado to this American way of being. What many of us are really saying outwardly is that we are too important, too critical to the enterprise, too necessary to our clients to possibly step away. So what would happen if we weren't there to answer every email and respond to every customer request for two weeks?

Newsflash: Life would go on.

When someone quits or drops dead, companies do not stop running. Even when it is the CEO.

So the feeble excuse that we are far too important or too devoted to our customers (I hear this one a lot from folks in professional services firms) to actually take a break now and then is egotistical nonsense.

But there is something darker at work here as well. We like the control. We like the power. We like to give ourselves a pat on the back for our commitment—we are so committed we are willing to make any and all sacrifices... sacrifices that are damaging to our health and vitality, and, even more importantly, that come at a huge cost both in the short term and the long term to our marriages, relationships with our children, and our souls.

> **The feeble excuse that we are far too important or too devoted to our customers to actually take a break now and then is egotistical nonsense.**

We know it is true and yet we continue to deceive ourselves with the misguided notion that this is just what is expected in corporate America today. And then we perpetuate this myth to the organizations we lead because we stubbornly refuse to role model anything differently. And the cycle continues.

My challenge to you is that it's possible to choose a different path. It's possible to train your boss to treat you differently.

My workaholic CEO boss did not invite me to take a two-week vacation where I was completely disconnected from the business. I didn't ask permission. I just did it—and did it in a way that supported the business and him in my absence... and let the clichéd chips fall where they may.

Was it risky? Yes. (I was back in the good-ol'-work-is-god-USA, no longer in Australia. It was definitely risky.)

Was I nervous the first time I did it? Yes. (Honestly, I didn't know if I could really do it, or if it would really work. It did.)

Did I wonder as I sipped cocktails and looked out at the Adriatic Sea if I had committed political suicide? Yes. (It was hard to remain worked up, since I was so blissed out, but the thought did cross my mind.)

But nothing bad happened. Not one thing. No one died. I wasn't fired. Nor was I sidelined and treated as though I wasn't "on the team." Life moved on. It was business as usual. And it can be for you too.

Take a deep breath, schedule that long overdue vacation, and prepare to unplug.

If you are afraid you'll be bored, use the time to fuel up in all four quadrants—heart, mind, body, and spirit. Revisit and clarify your Personal Declaration. Contemplate the next phase of your career. Express gratitude to the members of your pit crew who provide you with ongoing support.

See? You have plenty to accomplish!

You can thank me when you get back.

One final thought. A CEO of a $60 billion retailer, whom I advised recently, took a three-week unplugged holiday with his family. He is a public-company executive. If he can do it, why can't you?

11

Putting It All Together: You First

THIS SECTION HAS laid the foundation for you to consciously create a different, more fulfilling life for yourself by applying a few key principles and techniques. To recap how to lead your own fine self:

1. Self-awareness is essential. A great way to get fresh insight is to take a 360-degree survey.

2. Taking time to succinctly capture core information about who you are and what you stand for in your Personal Declaration is time well spent.

3. Being deliberate about creating and cultivating your personal pit crew is a game-changer.

4. Making a habit of getting in tune with yourself monthly by stepping on the Life Scale may be the single greatest method for taking control of your own fulfillment.

5. Managing your energy day to day by using deliberate rest and recharge periods is an easy way to increase your stamina and performance.

6. Clearly articulating where you want to be career-wise within a certain time frame is virtually a requirement for getting there.

7. Reframing how you view your career choices and consciously choosing experiences that broaden your expertise is critical, as is keeping your network close and informed along the way.

8. Being intentioned about the physical impression you make—your shtick—is important to being taken seriously and for professional advancement, whether you like it or not.

9. Receiving quality mentoring is as much about how you approach it as a mentee as it is about the mentor's expertise.

10. Not only do you need to take vacations, but knowing how to take them completely unplugged from work is essential for your overall health and well-being.

Some of the ideas shared in this section are easy life tweaks to make. Others may feel completely daunting and require enormous courage. My experience is that simply choosing to focus on one shift at a time is all it takes to start changing your life for the better. Remember the mantra: "Progress, not perfection... Progress, not perfection..."

PART
2

Lead Your Boss

ABOUT
"LEAD YOUR BOSS"

OVER THE COURSE of my career at three well-known global companies—Walmart, Campbell Soup Company, and Jim Beam (the liquor giant), I have worked for many bosses. Some good. Some fantastic. And some less than stellar. And I've been a boss too.

It ain't easy leading, and sometimes it certainly ain't easy following. Great followership requires many things. Most importantly, it requires great leadership—not from your boss but from you. It may sound cavalier to say that leadership is both an art and a science, but I believe it's true. I believe it's is even more the case when it comes to *leading your boss*.

Bosses are complicated creatures. They have power. They hold more information than you do. They go to meetings and discuss things that you will never know about. Depending on their style and your own family history, they can connect to feelings you may have about parents and authority. They can assume mythical proportions—especially if you don't know how to lead them effectively. Every day, they can be a source of ecstasy or agony.

> Great followership requires many things. Most importantly, it requires great leadership—not from your boss but from you.

Your relationship with your boss *does* require your leadership. Because the bottom line with bosses is that they want from you precisely what you want from your direct reports. In very practical terms, this section of the book translates your wishes for your own direct reports into seven simple techniques—one per chapter—to help you lead your boss and become a valued truth teller to them.

If you don't lead your own team, don't worry. Observing the principles and implementing the techniques described in the chapters that follow is probably your fastest way to advancement so that you *do* get to lead your own team someday.

Chapter 12 begins at the beginning—with you making the conscious and intentioned effort to get to know your boss in a meaningful way. To spend the time to try to understand who they are and how they are wired, so that you get off to a good start or reset your existing relationship.

Chapter 13 advocates a similar approach but in relationship to getting to know the business you are in. Taken together, mastering the advice in Chapters 12 and 13 creates a solid foundation for you to lead your boss—an approach that optimizes both your boss's acceptance of you and your positive impact on them.

Chapter 14 lays the groundwork for a solid working relationship, highlighting three basics you must deliver on in order to earn the right to lead your boss.

Chapter 15 shares a leadership accelerator that when applied ensures all your ideas and suggestions get the attention and respect they deserve.

Chapter 16 gives you a super-powerful yet simple tool for you to apply every week with your boss, ensuring that you become a trusted advisor and go-to team member.

Chapter 17 provides you with the first half of the "push back" equation that when expertly applied enables you to push back and challenge your boss and be heard.

Chapter 18 gives you the second half of the "push back" equation, along with expert tips on how to do just that.

Chapter 19 pulls it all together into a concise recap.

I know from experience that there's lots to be gained by reading and applying the ideas in this book—as long as you possess one essential attribute. What is that all-important quality? Compassion. (You thought I was going to say "courage," didn't you? You're going to need that too, but compassion is the inward motivator that will help you expertly demonstrate that courage.) And in this context, it means compassion for your boss.

Your boss has a bigger job than you do. Your boss has more people to manage. More responsibilities. More performance pressure. Your boss has what you have, multiplied several times over.

It is easy to forget all of that as you navigate the relationship with your boss. It is easy to judge, and to judge harshly. It is easy to maintain a laundry list of slights, grievances, and complaints.

That's also a waste of time.

"But Mindy, that's not fair!" you may be thinking. "My boss is a nightmare! He's an egomaniac who takes credit for my work." Or: "She's a political animal who doesn't care about the team but only about her own advancement." Or: "He is a moron." Or: "She's condescending and never listens to anyone else's ideas."

I could go on and on. I have encountered or experienced all of these attitudes and more. As have you. I know that bad bosses exist everywhere. And I know how painful it is to have one. I also know that all bosses have bad moments. The material in this section will enable you to navigate your experience better. Or, if you already enjoy a great relationship with your boss, it will help you improve it even more so that you get more of what you want, and it will reinforce how truth telling with your leader, when artfully applied, can absolutely transform your work life.

For as long as you choose to work for your boss, your job is to get in sync with that person—not the other way around. You will be successful by having a mindset and an approach to *make your boss successful.* It's very difficult to have compassion for your boss, and to recognize their humanity, if you are angry or resentful, clinging to unresolved hurts.

Imagine for a moment how wonderful you would feel if your direct reports had just read these paragraphs. Imagine them nodding enthusiastically, agreeing that *they* need to approach *you* with more compassion. They commit to acknowledging you as a fallible human being instead of judging you for being an imperfect leader. Because you *are* fallible, and so is your boss.

So, you have some choices to make. This section describes many opportunities you have to take an unconventional approach to interacting with your boss.

This approach will set you apart from your peers and yield amazingly positive responses from your boss—leaving you feeling fulfilled and energized (and likely promoted!).

The Courage Solution is not about giving your boss a pass. Rather, you need to make the decision to change yourself by *leading* your boss as a truth teller. When you start leading your boss, you will have the best chance of creating the positive change you desire. You can't change your boss, but you can always change how you *engage* your boss. When you do that, everything around you will also change, and change for the better.

12

Demystifying the Big Dawg

M Y FIRST BOSS in corporate America went by the moniker "Bubba." He was, by far, the worst boss of my career.

In the Introduction to this section, I urged you to have compassion for your boss and acknowledge your boss's humanity. That's all good stuff. But it is hard to have compassion for someone if you don't understand how they are wired or why they are wired the way they are.

My failure to "decode" Bubba early in our relationship—especially since I was fresh from actively seeing patients as a psychotherapist—makes me shake my head to this day. I was so busy jumping into learning my job that I didn't pause long enough to get a read on him. Instead, I learned the hard way—by pushing all of his personal hot buttons in my first weeks of working for him.

SHARE YOUR PERSONAL DECLARATION

YOUR FIRST JOB when you join an organization is figuring out who's who in the zoo—starting with your boss—and getting a read on them. But crawling into the psyche of your boss can be challenging.

I recently heard someone talking about their new boss, trying to figure him out. This senior leader went on about how the boss talked a lot about transparency yet was anything but transparent himself. The senior leader had been working for that boss for nearly nine months. What had taken him so long? You need to demystify the big dawg far sooner than that!

One of the best ways of accelerating this demystifying process is to schedule a 1:1 early on in your relationship so you can share your Personal Declaration. As I discuss in Chapter 2 in Part 1, "You First," a Personal Declaration is your succinct sharing of the following:

- Your family of origin (where you grew up, details about your siblings and parents).

- Your family now.

- Your strengths and weaknesses.

- What motivates you/fuels you.

- Your values.

- Your leadership philosophy.

- Your pet peeves.

Essentially, it is taking time to openly share your core self with another person. And it is something I suggest you do very soon with your boss (and your direct reports, if you have any) when you start a new job. Equally important, *invite them to reciprocate*.

One of my bosses was absolutely flabbergasted by my openness, especially since we had just started working together. But I was unconcerned by his reaction. The fact that he hadn't experienced such openness before didn't mean the conversation wasn't valuable. Over time he could determine whether what I disclosed about myself lined up with my actions. And because I shared with him the topics above, he responded during our conversation by sharing details about his early years growing up and other personal details that helped me understand him better (and have more compassion for him when I was frustrated with him!).

Several years later, he asked me how I was doing after I'd just returned from a grueling multi-week around-the-world trip visiting our various businesses. He said, "Mindy, are you rested? How have you been sleeping? I remember you telling me when we first started working together that getting a good night's sleep is something that is important to your well-being. Are you getting enough sleep these days given your schedule?"

This took me by surprise because he had never directly referenced our Personal Declaration session before. But now he was asking sincerely about something that I had shared with him early in our working relationship.

When you have the courage for that type of conversation with your boss—and then ask your boss to share similar information with you—you are actively attempting to get to know them quickly so that you can create a good operating rhythm. Don't just seek surface-level information. Get curious about their family of origin. About their story. It will be of incalculable value to you over time.

It's especially useful to learn how your new boss is wired. Ask them whom you could speak with to find this out. Most leaders are amused by this bold request but also very happy to direct you to people who can provide this perspective. Your boss will appreciate your doing your homework, as it speaks to your desire to be prepared and informed.

GATHER INTEL

AN EFFECTIVE WAY to get to know your boss, even before you join the company or department, is to gather intel. Those who are interviewing you as you progress through the interview process are excellent sources of information on your prospective boss. You can also reach out to your network to find someone who might know your potential boss.

Ask these people how they would describe the boss's decision making, conflict resolution, and whatever else comes to mind. Here's a list of the types of questions you should be asking both prior to working for someone and once you've been hired:

- Greatest strengths?

- Greatest weaknesses?

- Pet peeves or hot buttons?

- Sacred cows (the untouchable topics at work)?

- What types of behavior get rewarded?

- How do they get their energy or inspiration?

- What is something most people don't know about them?

- How do they make their decisions?

- What are their working habits and what is the optimal time to approach them?

- Who's in their inner circle and why?

- How do they resolve conflict among team members?

- How do they behave when they are angry?

- What is their preferred style of communication—formal or informal (e.g., preprinted agendas are required for all meetings or informal "flybys" are more their style)?

This list is by no means exhaustive, but it's a good start.

After you finish gathering this information, you need to directly ask your boss a subset of these same questions:

- How do you characterize your signature strength?

- What do you consider your greatest weakness?

- How do you like to communicate (email, text, phone)?

- How often/what cadence do you prefer for staying connected (monthly 1:1s, a weekly touch base, a daily "drive-by")?

- What are your pet peeves?

- What motivates you? Why do you come to work every day?

- How and when do you prefer to be challenged (anytime or in private only; mornings are best or never before noon)?

- What do you wish every direct report knew about you?

UNDERSTAND WHAT MOTIVATES YOUR BOSS

ONE OF THE most important things to know about your boss is what *truly* motivates them. That is the key to understanding how they get energy and where they like to spend their time. Even if you have already asked them outright, you may not truly know until you've observed them in action for at least a few months.

One of my bosses adored the numbers. He would wake up every day and right away look at the sales reports. No matter which direction the numbers were headed, he was absolutely jazzed to be going to work to impact them. Those numbers motivated him even though he was by then very senior and had larger strategic issues to wrestle with.

> One of the most important things to know about your boss is what *truly* motivates them.

Another boss was cheerful and easy to deal with when he returned from visiting teams in our various markets. After a week of market visits, he was 100 percent happy, fueled up, and able to deal with the daily grind. Being in the market gave him energy.

I get motivated by feeling like I'm making a tangible difference in someone's life. After all the work, meetings, decisions, and general busyness that make up a C-suite executive's daily life, it's the feeling that a meaningful conversation or practical decision positively impacted an individual or a group of people that really motivates me.

LOOK PAST THE BOSS FAÇADE

AND FINALLY, TRY to see past the boss façade to find the person behind the title. I had one boss who was incredibly challenging. There were moments when the only thing that stopped me from quitting on the spot, or telling him to shove it where the sun doesn't shine, was remembering that trapped inside that adult frame was a little boy whose father had abandoned him. Knowing that helped me find a smidgen of compassion in those moments when he was draining me with his brand of crazy.

> Figuring out your boss to the best of your ability early on is to your advantage. That's not so you can judge them but so that you can determine the best way to work in partnership.

Human beings are by their very nature a hot mess. A boss's basic humanity can become amplified—whether positively or negatively. Figuring out your boss to the best of your ability early on is to your advantage. That's not so you can judge them but so that you can determine the best way to work in partnership. This is essential for applying the principles discussed in Chapters 14 to 18.

Just as you've mapped the territory of your boss, you need to do the same for your company by getting clear on the fundamentals of the business. We'll take a look at how to do this in Chapter 13.

13

Win over Your Boss by Thinking like an Owner

WHENEVER YOU EMBARK on an ambitious journey, it's important to have a map. But it's also important to remember, as the Polish-American philosopher Alfred Korzybski said, that "the map is not the territory." A map provides an idea of the landscape and important landmarks you will encounter but doesn't tell you what it will look and feel like when you are experiencing it firsthand.

The same is true for work.

When you first start at a company or take on a new role, it is essential to your overall success on the job—and to your success with your boss in particular—for you to take the time up front to create your own company "map" so that you can more easily navigate the landscape at work. While you will likely gather basic information about your particular department or general facts about the company overall, if you fail to deliberately map the territory, you lose valuable early momentum.

Now, I suspect you're going to say, "Mindy, I already know this stuff." And you probably do. My challenge to you is to not just know it but to act on it. To actually *do* something with what you know. To have it influence how you problem solve at work.

If you are a CEO or C-suite executive, go ahead and jump to Chapter 14. You already live, eat, sleep, and breathe the content I am about to share, every day of the company you lead. But for everyone else, read this chapter through to the end. Go on—humor me.

My experience in the corporate world over 20 years has proven to me time and again that most business professionals don't know what I'm about to share. Or if they do, it's not reflected in their thinking or the solutions they propose to business issues. You'll have to see if you agree with that after you've read the chapter.

> Mapping the territory at work—especially when you first start at a company or take on a new role—is essential to your overall success on the job.

KNOW THE COMPANY PURPOSE

IT ALL STARTS with knowing the company purpose. To get started, answer this question about your company:

Why does your company exist (what is its purpose)?

Every day, from minute one, you need to understand what your company does and why.

Simple, right? At Jim Beam, we existed to make and sell spirits.

If I wanted to go a bit deeper into our purpose, I'd say it was to caretake spirits brands that were decades or even centuries old, and to ensure that the heritage and quality of the brands were preserved for generations to come.

That was the easy question. The second question is equally important, but answering it fully may be a bit more challenging:

How does your company make money?

_____

_____

_____

_____

_____

_____

You need to be able to follow a dollar bill all the way from a customer's hands to your company's bank account. Do you know how that happens? Take a look at your answer above. Likely, it is incomplete.

Let me take you through a simple illustration.

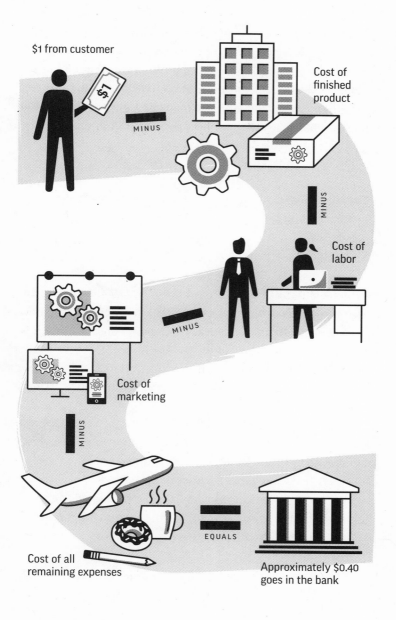

$1 from customer

MINUS

Cost of finished product

MINUS

Cost of labor

MINUS

Cost of marketing

MINUS

Cost of all remaining expenses

EQUALS

Approximately $0.40 goes in the bank

This example is basic, but it sheds light on how the company operates and how the pieces fit together. And, in case you didn't notice, it is a basic walk through the P&L (profit and loss) statement from the top line (revenue) to bottom-line profit (income).*

Your ability to map this out for your company yourself is essential because it will force you to know:

- Your end customer.

- What it costs to actually make the product or service your company sells.

- What it costs to market the product or service.

- How much your company spends on overhead (people, physical infrastructure, general expenses).

- The company's average profit margins.

- The purpose of all the company's departments and functions.

When you know these things, you can begin to think like a CEO. With this knowledge, you are well equipped to make good decisions no matter your role or level in the company.

Several years ago, when I was working at Jim Beam, we had a group of six summer interns who I absolutely adored. We hired them for various marketing and sales roles. I met with this group every month, and at our initial meeting I gave them a homework

---

* For you finance folks, I know I am skipping EBITDA and other technical items here. Trying to illustrate a point, not teach a full P&L lesson.

assignment, to be completed before they could "graduate" from their internship.

The assignment was to present the P&L to our group in a way that compellingly illustrated their understanding of how the company made money and their role in that process.

These kids were smart. They all had business degrees from great universities. But they found this assignment challenging. They really had to dig in, ask a bunch of questions of a lot of different people, and connect the dots themselves. Their confidence skyrocketed after completing this exercise because they now had a mental map of how the business operated. It gave them context and perspective.

Later, after we had hired them into full-time marketing and sales roles, they told me how their own bosses didn't really understand how everything fit together and how to break down the P&L. Their view was that every employee should have to go through that exercise because it was such an eye-opener.

It's all too easy to jump right into a job and focus only on your own responsibilities or those of your department, without ever pulling back and looking holistically at the business. But doing this as part of the mapping exercise is critical (you'll find a cheat sheet at the end of the chapter where you can do it yourself).

KNOW THE ECOSYSTEM

KNOWING HOW YOUR department fits into the company ecosystem is another key element of mapping the territory.

Is your company organized by business units or functions or geographies?

Does your company operate as a matrix?

Is your company a sales-led organization? Or R&D? Or brand-led? Or other?

Where does the power and influence reside?

What functions are mission-centric?

The answers to these questions provide context for decoding how decisions are made, resources are allocated, and trade-offs are determined.

Early in my tenure at Jim Beam, I gave some remarks at a quarterly town hall meeting that was live webcast to our thousands of employees around the world, along with the hundreds of people at headquarters. I pointed out that our company's purpose was to make and sell spirits, that certain functions directly involved in that purpose (manufacturing, marketing, R&D, and sales) were "mission critical," and that other functions (including finance, IT, HR, legal, and supply chain) were support. Those basic facts would influence how we made investment decisions in employee development and in other ways.

Later, an IT leader told me he was offended because I hadn't listed IT as mission critical. I explained that IT was certainly important, but being world class at IT was not going to significantly increase shareholder value creation. But world-class distillers, marketers, and sales folks would be game-changing for us.

I also said that if he wanted to be mission critical, he needed to go work for an IT-services firm. He didn't particularly appreciate that comment, but he got my point.

KNOW HOW YOUR DEPARTMENT FITS IN

UNDERSTANDING THE TOTAL enterprise is one thing. Understanding the department you work in and how it connects with the overall purpose and strategy of the company is another. Make sure you know the long-term strategy of the company, the annual priorities overall, and the priorities and focus areas of your department. This is essential for your success.

If these things don't seem to line up with the posters on the wall, so to speak, it's time to start asking questions.

One senior executive tells every person who works for her that there are five numbers to always know about their business. She shared with me that those five numbers are different for each person depending on their area, and that they may change depending on the meeting the person is in and whom they are speaking to. But the discipline of being rooted in five core metrics is the starting point. For instance, her head of R&D needs to be able to talk in detail and coherently at all times about:

- Number of innovation projects

- Operating expenses and headcount budget

- Timeline dates for launch of major products

- Formulation cost makeup of major brands

- Growth performance of major brands

A brand leader in a consumer packaged-goods company might need to always know:

- Current market share of the product

- Current shipments

- Sales required to hit balance of year targets

- Growth of key competitors

- Growth of the product category

This executive told me that being given this same advice early in her career has served her well. Indeed, she is now a global chief marketing officer and has led a $2 billion business.

KNOW THE CULTURE

GETTING AN EARLY and quick read on how things are really done in the company, and what the corporate ethos is, will help you navigate effectively. Some companies value courageous leadership. Others encourage collaborative leadership. And yet others place a premium on getting stuff done quickly, process be damned.

Being crystal clear about how decisions get made, what behaviors are really valued (no matter what the posters on the wall say or what corporate slogans are thrown around), and "how we do things around here" will give you an advantage over your colleagues.

Why?

Because if you know the culture and can name it, you can adapt to it and work within the system to move things ahead (as opposed to being stymied by it). Sharing the best ideas with your boss will have no value if you can't implement them.

SO, WHAT DOES THIS HAVE TO DO
WITH LEADING YOUR BOSS?

IN ORDER FOR you to have coherent dialogue and debate with your boss, and for your suggestions and ideas to truly add value, you must have an enterprise-wide mindset. When you do that, you can think like an owner. You can act as if every dollar spent is your own dollar.

When you approach issues and problem resolution from a perspective broader than your individual or departmental view, yet also know your area cold and can anticipate and answer questions about your scope of responsibility, you demonstrate business leadership. That shows maturity. And wisdom. And it will elevate every conversation you have with your boss. It may actually help your boss lead better.

> **Your voice will rise above others when you are prepared and know your key metrics.**

And keep in mind it will be difficult for your boss to see you as a valued truth teller if you don't have all the facts.

Your boss will value your ideas if they are framed within the broad context of your company's purpose. Your voice will rise above others when you are prepared and know your key metrics. And you are far more likely to get promoted faster than your peers if your knowledge and action fits within the culture of the company and "the way we do things around here."

Now it's your turn. Complete the cheat sheet below and then think about how this knowledge can influence how you are approaching your job.

MAPPING THE TERRITORY CHEAT SHEET

Why your company exists (its purpose): _____

_____

_____

_____

HOW YOUR COMPANY MAKES MONEY, AND HOW
YOU MAKE A DIFFERENCE

FOLLOW THE DOLLAR *Write here the numbers for your company's overall P&L.*	HOW I IMPACT THE BUSINESS *Capture here what you do specifically that impacts the business enterprise-wide.*
$ from our customer: _____ (total annual revenue/sales) (our customer is _____).	*Am I in a department or role that directly interfaces with our end customer (e.g., sales)?*
The cost of producing our product/service: _____ (cost of goods sold—COGS)	*Am I in a department or role that creates any element of the product or service?*
The cost of all operating expenses, including the employees: _____ (operating expenses—OPEX)	*What decisions do I make that impact how money is spent and the amount? If I owned this company, would I be happy with what I spent?*
What is left to go in the bank: _____ (operating income—OI)	*What is our operating margin compared with the margins of our competitors?*

Your company strategy and the key priorities: _____

_____

_____

_____

_____

_____

_____

Your company ecosystem—four factors in how the company is organized:

1. *The company is organized by (business units, functions, geographies, other):* _____

   _____

   _____

2. *Does your company operate as a matrix?* Yes ____ No ____

3. *Is your company a sales-led organization? Or R&D? Or brand-led? Other?* _____

   _____

   _____

4. *Where does the power and influence reside? What functions are mission-centric?* _____

   _____

   _____

The five critical numbers I always need to know and why:

1. _____
   _____

2. _____
   _____

3. _____
   _____

4. _____
   _____

5. _____
   _____

Our company culture—how things really work (in your own words—not the corporate slogans): _____
_____
_____
_____
_____
_____
_____

14

The Price of Admission

WHENEVER I TELL someone in the business world to be the follower they wish their own direct reports would be, they hesitate and then say, "Oh yeah. That's a really good way to think about it." Most don't do it, though. It's so easy to look at your leader and count the numerous failings. Yet you forget that your direct reports are doing the exact same thing when they look at you.

One of the best ways to lead your boss—and to enjoy a fantastic, mutually respectful relationship—is to treat them exactly the way you would want to be treated.

Do you wish the people on your team were more prepared with facts and alternatives when they enter your office to discuss something?

Your leader wishes the same thing about you.

Do you wish your team would anticipate problems rather than getting caught flat-footed when the stuff hits the fan?

Your boss has probably wished the same thing about you.

Do you wish your team would consistently deliver on promises and commitments?

Ditto for how your leader feels about you.

See how this works?

While you are wishing your boss would get their act together and be a better leader, your boss is wishing you would get your act together and be a better follower. Keeping this firmly in mind will help you do the three important things that are essential for building a great relationship with your boss:

Inform early and often.

When you mess up, 'fess up.

Give the benefit of the doubt to your boss.

These principles are the "price of admission" to creating a solid relationship with your leader. And yes, they require a measure of courage.

INFORM EARLY AND OFTEN

NO LEADER LIKES to be surprised. Ever. And you don't either, right?

"Inform early and often" is pretty basic advice—it falls in the category of You-Gotta-Nail-the-Basics when it comes to having a great relationship with your boss.

Don't be passive. Proactively share information—certainly the good stuff but especially the bad. Do not wait to be asked about negative numbers or a negative trend or any difficulty with a project. Every time you do that, you erode trust.

> One of the best ways to lead your boss is to treat them exactly the way you would want to be treated.

One of the peers I worked with for many years made this mistake often. He would enthusiastically and quickly race to our boss to share great monthly or quarterly results but was nowhere to be found when the numbers were flat or negative. This drove our boss crazy. He would then have to hunt my colleague down for an explanation on what was going on with the business, and then my colleague would complain that he was being micromanaged. He could have eliminated all that static had he been consistent in informing our leader early and often no matter what was going on with the numbers.

> **Do not wait to be asked about negative numbers or a negative trend or any difficulty with a project. Every time you do that, you erode trust.**

WHEN YOU MESS UP, 'FESS UP

MISTAKES WILL BE made. You, members of the team you are on, and those you may lead are imperfect human beings. Problems are inevitable. What isn't inevitable is an apology. Business professionals are quick to point out that mistakes are being made all the time at their organization. They always laugh when I ask, "When was the last time someone at work apologized to you?"

The follow-up question, of course, is "When was the last time you apologized?"

An apology on either side is a rare occurrence. I remind these leaders that no one is walking on water.

Let's review the three elements of a great apology (see Chapter 23 in Part 3, "Lead Your Peers," for more on this).

- Actually saying "I'm sorry" out loud—while making eye contact, if possible.

- Acknowledging your error by adding the phrase "I was wrong... but more importantly, you were right" (add the second part only if that is in fact the case).

- Asking humbly, "How can I fix this?"

Be aware that an effective apology requires you to have actually begun working on a solution by the time you get to step 3. Otherwise you're just dumping the problem in your boss's lap.

Stating clearly how you (and your team) are in the process of coming up with a solution will build confidence. Your leader will be impressed by your forthrightness, maturity, and initiative. They may still be ticked off or frustrated or disappointed, but it will be about the issues and not about you.

An article entitled "When Senior Managers Won't Collaborate," in the March 2015 edition of *Harvard Business Review*, presented evidence that many business leaders tend to blame mistakes on anyone except their own teams. While this is unsurprising given human nature, it is disheartening. But imagine how you would stand out among your peers by accepting accountability instead of looking for a scapegoat.

Bottom line? When you (or the team you lead) have made a mistake, your boss wants to hear it from you and not from someone else. Own up to it, deal with it directly, and communicate progress as you work through the issue.

GIVE THE BENEFIT OF THE DOUBT TO YOUR BOSS

GIVING YOUR LEADER the benefit of the doubt can be tremendously challenging at times, but it helps to do so because your boss does have more stress than you have. They have a bigger job than you. They have more performance pressure than you. That is just the reality of it, as you read in the Introduction to this section.

I'll never forget the night this truth registered with me. I was one month into my job as global chief human resources officer at Jim Beam and I was embarrassed to admit to myself that I had naively minimized the scale, scope, and challenge of this role. When I was at Campbell Soup Company, I would find myself frustrated at the pace of decision making or issue resolution. At the time, I didn't appreciate the complexity involved—the multiple stakeholders who needed to be

> **It always looks easier from the outside—just wait until you sit in the chair.**

addressed and the myriad other responsibilities that were invisible to me but a reality for my then boss who held the role I now occupied.

Recalling this was a good reminder as I dealt with my new boss at Jim Beam that I needed to be more patient and keep in mind that his world was more complex than mine. Undoubtedly there were reasons he navigated issues the way he did that I wouldn't understand.

It always looks easier from the outside—just wait until you sit in the chair.

. . . And to Everyone Else You Work With

Although it might be tempting to gain short-lived political favor by throwing your colleagues under the bus, doing so erodes your credibility with your boss over the long term. Your leader is looking for a balanced perspective. For maturity. For wisdom. Just like you want from the people you lead.

Don't get sucked into saying negative things about others you work with, even if your boss is venting to you about them. The old adage "If you can't say anything nice, don't say anything at all" comes to mind here. Listen respectfully. And answer direct questions with balanced feedback, remembering how you would want to be treated if a colleague was asked about you.

ONE FINAL THOUGHT

THE PRINCIPLES DISCUSSED in this chapter are neither groundbreaking nor new. They are, however, the "price of admission" to creating a solid relationship with your leader. To choose to not abide by these principles is to abdicate your responsibility as a follower. You are annoyed and disappointed if your direct reports fail to do these things. And conversely, you are delighted and appreciative when they do.

Your leader is no different. You can hardly lead your boss effectively and become a valued truth teller if you cannot master yourself and your ego—which is really what these principles require of you.

15

Supercharge Your Solutions

WHEN I WAS a psychotherapist, my job was to put myself out of work. The point was not to have my patients unendingly need me but to be a thought partner with them for a short period. I wanted to help them make a positive shift or successfully address a specific issue.

Fast-forward to what feels like a lifetime later. When I was at Jim Beam, I had a discussion with my team following my annual "mountaintop retreat"—when I went off to think deeply for a few days about the state of the business, the company strategy, where we'd been, where we were headed, our shared purpose, and my leadership effectiveness.

When I returned to the office, I posed the following to my leadership team:

Imagine a world where the leaders at our company were so strong and skilled that they no longer needed the human resources function. What would it take to put our entire function out of a job?

The debate and discussion that ensued led to our team embarking on an 18-month journey intensely focused on two things:

1. Strengthening our senior leaders to operate more independently and deliver the strategy of the company.

2. Completely revamping our global function to make it more effective, which included reducing our cost to the company by 40 percent, so that money could be reinvested in brand building.

If each of us as business leaders imagined ourselves as CEO of the company, we would want strong leaders who could effectively lead their people while delivering shareholder value, with money and resources targeted at the mission-critical areas of the business. Back-office functions should be lean and low-cost, and operate with laser-like focus on strategy delivery.

This is what I call "king for a day" thinking.

IF YOU WERE KING FOR A DAY

THE MOST EFFECTIVE way of getting to the heart of a business problem is to step back and ask yourself, "If I were king for a day, given all the information that I have, what would I decide?"

This question will completely transform how you approach problems and find solutions. It forces you to step outside your job title or department and instead think enterprise-wide.

Myopic thinking in business is a huge issue. You see it during the annual budget cycle, in strategic planning, and in basic intra-department squabbling. So if you want to stand out as a go-to person for your boss, offer solutions to problems that are a win for the company, not just for your department. Start by returning to the fundamentals you articulated in the cheat sheet at the end of Chapter 13 and do a sense check:

How does this solution serve the overall purpose of the company?

In what way does this answer lead to greater shareholder value creation?

If you were running this company, where would you put your resources in order to deliver sustainable, profitable growth?

When I was working at Campbell Soup Company, a "king for a day" approach was taken at a team meeting focused on resource allocation. One of the function leaders announced to his peers, "I will reduce my operating budget by 15 percent and give that dollar amount to the business-unit president, who can use it to grow our top line. That's better use of our company cash."

> **If you want to stand out as a go-to person for your boss, offer solutions to problems that are a win for the company, not just for your department.**

The response from teammates was immediate and profound. All of a sudden, everyone began to think more creatively, offering solutions that benefited the company holistically, as opposed to protecting their own budgets.

What do you think the boss's reaction was to that leader? Pretty impressed.

NO SEAT AT THE TABLE? THINK AGAIN.

ONE OF THE excuses for inaction that irks me the most is "But I don't have a seat at the table." In other words, you are not listened to, or you are not treated with the same consideration as others in the group. This may be true, but I believe there is a straightforward solution. In short, participate in team discussions as if you were king for a day. This is where you really test your business knowledge and understanding of how your company operates and makes money.

During team discussions, imagine that you run the company and offer solutions based on that premise. You have the same fact set or data that everyone else has—same P&L, business reports, and so on. You know the strategy and mission of the company, so you can deduce which areas are mission critical. You know the annual financial goals. You know the risks and challenges facing the business. And if you don't know the answer to any of these, it is your job to find them out.

Business is largely common sense. Grounding yourself in the facts and then thinking critically about the issues confronting the company—as if you were in charge—will free you to offer much better suggestions than you otherwise might. Many times I have felt inspired to challenge a business leader after simply asking myself, "If I were king for a day, what would I do?" That mindset is a confidence and courage driver.

There is no excuse for not contributing during meetings. It is not your boss's job to get you up to speed. That's your job. Which means you have to care. This requires both your head and your heart.

Consistently demonstrate the "king for a day" approach to your business and you will be delighted with the response you get when you speak up and contribute. Your leader will be far more likely to support your requests or ideas. And you will be far more engaged and connected, and have a greater sense of meaning and purpose. You will feel valued— because you are adding real value.

WHEN MY TEAM invited our CEO to discuss our idea of putting our function "out of business," he was astounded. Most of all, he was impressed with the group's maturity and approach. The team's focus on helping the company in a significant way while putting aside its desire to protect its turf enabled a healthy discussion and debate.

Companies need more people, and more executives in particular, who can put forward solutions that reach beyond their own department (and beyond the next quarter). These employees will be most likely to put the company's interests above narrow-minded concerns related to how the company pie gets sliced. Their focus is on building a bigger pie. If you can be that person—the "pie grower" and not the "pie slicer"— your career prospects will improve and your company will be better positioned to achieve long-term growth.

> Companies need more people, and more executives in particular, who can put forward solutions that reach beyond their own department (and beyond the next quarter).

16

Getting on the Same Wavelength

THERE IS ONE relationship that makes or breaks how you feel about going to the office every day and also determines whether you stay at the company.

You know who it's with.

It's what this entire section is about.

Your boss.

The writer Eric Bloom has remarked on something that I have found to be true throughout my career: "People join companies and leave managers." This observation was borne out by a recent survey of the top 10 reasons people hate their jobs, described in a LinkedIn post.* Reason number 1 was (and I'm quoting here): "Their boss sucks." In 2013, when Gallup conducted a poll of 150,000 workers, 70 percent did not like their job or their boss. In 2014, a majority of employees, 51 percent, were still "not engaged" and 17.5 percent were "actively disengaged."†

---

* Ilya Pozin, "The Top 10 Reasons People Hate Their Job," *LinkedIn Pulse*, July 9, 2013.

† Amy Adkins, "Majority of U.S. Employees Not Engaged Despite Gains in 2014," *Gallup*, January 28, 2015.

What can *you* do if that survey describes your experience right now? What can *you* do if your relationship with your leader is less than stellar?

Remember, the only thing you can reliably control or change at your company is yourself. And there is a payoff for doing so, I promise you. So before you leave your manager, consider the happiness-driver tool described below.

THE TRANSFORMATIONAL POWER OF A QUESTION

WHEN I LEFT Jim Beam, I was the CEO's right-hand man, despite being the only female on the executive team. He gave me freedom to get my job done. He and I were partners and mutual challengers. We were in a great place.

But it had not always been this way. Four and a half years earlier, our relationship was a disaster. I was miserable, and after several months on the job, I wanted to quit because we were completely out of sync. I felt micromanaged, not listened to, and as if nothing I did was ever good enough.

I thought I had tried everything—which really just meant working longer and longer and harder and harder—and yet nothing changed. I also got in the terrible habit of complaining and venting about my boss.

Then, late one night, I was sitting in my office long after everyone else had left. I was on speakerphone with Michael,* my coach in Australia. I was venting. Again. (It had, unfortunately, become a monthly occurrence since I had moved back to the

---

* If you've read Part 1, "You First," you know about Michael Hall. He is the brilliant founder and CEO of WildWorks, a business and leadership consultancy based in Sydney, Australia. And yes, you guessed it—an essential part of my personal pit crew.

United States.) I vented about how stressed I was, how exhausted I was, and how I couldn't possibly work any harder. I was thinking about quitting.

Michael stopped me mid-rant and said the most profound yet simple thing: "Mindy, your boss is not going to change. The only way to get back in control of your life is for *you* to change."

"But *I'm* not the problem," I retorted. "My boss is. Why should I have to be the one to change?"

"Mate—do you want to be happy or do you want to quit?" he asked.

Ding!

The light bulb finally went on.

In all my busyness and racing around and self-righteous indignation, I had forgotten the one truism in life and in business: that the *only* thing I could reliably change was me. And that meant, no matter what he was like as a leader, it was *my job* to get in sync with my boss. Not the other way around. What I was doing was not working. Period. So either I was going to change or I was going to quit.

I chose to change.

Here's what I changed: I stopped judging my leader and started to intentionally look for things I liked and respected about him—and focused my mind only on those things. I went on a *no complaining* diet. And I stopped reminiscing about "the good old days" and how awesome my former boss had been.

I had chosen to move to Chicago and leave my life in Australia behind. I was here now. I was accountable for the life I was creating.

AS I CONSCIOUSLY *chose a different way to feel toward my boss,* I was reminded of how we tend to minimize the difficulty of a boss's job. Rationally, we know they have more people to manage. More priorities. More pressure. More deliverables. More. More. More. But human nature means we don't focus on that. In fact, research indicates that most people believe they can do their boss's job better than the boss can. So it's likely you now are thinking exactly that about your leader!

It's not until you personally experience the transition of taking a big promotion and stepping into your boss's job that your mentality shifts. Why? Because then you are on the hook for more. Then you are accountable for more. More pressure. More people to manage. More priorities. More deliverables. More. More. More.

Once I got my head back on straight, Michael recommended that I do something every week to engage differently with my boss. My homework assignment was to ask my boss at the end of each week, "What is your single greatest priority over the coming week?"

> When you get in tune with what your boss needs and focus there first, other areas of your work will flow easier—freeing up time and capacity.

Michael explained that consistently asking my boss this question would help me get into his head. It would illuminate what he was worried about, so I could start bringing him the solutions that he needed. As a result of this, Michael counseled, my boss and I would *naturally fall into greater alignment.*

Imagine how beneficial it would be if your direct reports and the project teams you lead asked about your single greatest priority each week so that they could bring solutions to the problems you are wrestling with.

That would be awesome, right? So now, if you start doing the same thing, imagine the impact it will have on your relationship with your boss.

INSTEAD OF TRYING to get my boss to listen to me, I focused on *fully* listening to him first. That's when the magic started to happen and our relationship began to change. The more in tune I became with him and the more I showed my sincere desire to support him by bringing ideas and solutions, the more he listened to me and sought me out for my advice and perspective.

This ultimately led to me becoming his go-to executive on our leadership team. Not because I was smarter than my peers. I certainly wasn't. Not because I cared more about the business than they did. We had a rock-star team and we were all in it to win it. Not because I was supremely diplomatic. I definitely wasn't.

It was because he could count on me to be oriented primarily toward his agenda, and aligned to his issues and concerns.

Q&A
· · · · ·

Mindy, I get the part about not being so judgmental and being more empathetic because my boss has a bigger job than I do. But she will think I'm a weirdo if I start asking her this question out of the blue.
You're right in that it will be different. But maybe your boss will read this and then try to figure out the best way to approach *her* boss with the same question. Bottom line? Don't worry if at first you feel awkward or unsure. Just ask. And then listen.

You're trying to develop a better understanding of what is happening in the business. Over time it will become a natural part of how you engage with your boss. She'll become accustomed to you bringing ideas about and solutions for the issues that matter most.

Mindy, I'm honestly feeling overwhelmed right now. I have way too much work to get done as it is. I have no personal life, and now you are telling me to go ask my boss this question so that I can do more work?

Asking your boss about their greatest priority will not increase your workload. In fact, it will actually diminish in your life a little something I call "grind." You know what grind is—that experience at work where everything you try to accomplish is difficult. You just feel like you are grinding it out, day in and day out. Not fun.

When you get in tune with what your boss needs and focus there first, other areas of your work will flow easier—freeing up time and capacity. I found that once I shifted to this new way of behaving, I started working less—and with far less grind.

But what if my boss is simply wrong? What if I fundamentally disagree with my boss even though I like my boss as a person?

In order to be genuinely heard on any issue, especially when it involves very sensitive or strongly held beliefs that your boss has and you disagree with, you need to first build the relationship. You have to focus your time and attention on them, so that it's more about them than about you—so that, in turn, they can hear you when you challenge them. You must build a wellspring of goodwill in order to courageously challenge and be heard (see Chapters 17 and 18 for more on this).

HERE'S THE DEAL, though. Once I finally got into the driver's seat of my relationship with my boss, he didn't suddenly transform into a beautiful combination of Pope Francis and Warren Buffett. He was the same well-intentioned albeit complicated person.

And I was still the opinionated, intense, deeply flawed person I am.

This is not a personality makeover. This is not about liking each other. My leader liked me fine (I think). I liked him fine. He was fun to chat with at work dinners. We just hadn't been on the same wavelength on the job. And that got in the way of everything.

Through my owning that I could change *only* myself and how I engaged with him, our relationship changed. For the better.

No matter what your relationship is with your boss right now, you can improve it. Dramatically.

You can do that through your willingness to *change your mindset and attitude*—by remembering that *your boss has far more responsibility, stress, and pressure than you do*—and by *actively checking in with your leader every week*, and asking the magic question about their single greatest priority for the coming days *so that you can provide solutions*. When you do this, I guarantee that change—for the better for *you*—will occur.

You must build a well-spring of goodwill in order to courageously challenge and be heard

When you are in sync with your boss, your work life is automatically more enjoyable regardless of what's going on—reorganizations, changes in strategy, budget tightening, acquisitions, divestitures, anything!

If you are in sync with your boss, you just are happier. And you go home happier. Which is good for everyone.

17

Stroke, Stroke...

W HEN I WAS in graduate school studying to become a
marriage and family therapist, one of my professors
taught me a therapeutic method known as "stroke, stroke,
kick." The basic concept is that people don't like to change. Even
if they show up in your office and pay you for your help, they
still don't like it when you challenge their belief system. Which
is a pretty fundamental thing to do for successful psychotherapy.

So you employ the stroke, stroke, kick method—which means
looking for ways to support and offer affirmation to the client
twice as often as you challenge or "kick" them.

I am going to share how the stroke part of this method
works on the job with your boss. We'll get to the kick in the next
chapter.

This method is applicable not only to your boss, but it's
included in this section—rather than in "Lead Your Team" or
"Lead Your Peers"—because I've noticed that most people do a
fairly good job of providing positive feedback and commentary
to teams and peers—at least in comparison with what they provide to their boss.

I'm often struck by the general lack of affirmation, support, gratitude, and encouragement shown to a boss. It's almost as if people think their boss doesn't need it—that the boss is invincible or perhaps getting affirmation elsewhere.

But the opposite is true. Yes, the more senior a person gets, the more ego stroking and ass kissing they receive—while receiving less and less authentic praise, support, and encouragement. This is a trend that needs to be reversed.

Not only is the ego-stroking approach disingenuous, but it propagates the "emperor has no clothes" phenomenon that occurs with many leaders. No one tells them the truth and really challenges them (the "kick"). Yet they are constantly being sucked up to.

> **You cannot get a positive response or change or shift from a well-placed kick if you have not first provided genuine strokes.**

But you cannot get a positive response or change or shift from a well-placed kick if you have not first provided genuine strokes.

THREE SIMPLE WAYS TO PROVIDE GENUINE AFFIRMATION

IN ORDER TO provide genuine strokes, you really need to have the right mindset. You need a heartfelt intention to look for ways to encourage your boss and affirm their actions. This can be incredibly difficult if you find yourself saddled with a loathsome creature for a leader. But if you *seek* to find something—just one thing—that you admire or respect about your boss, that one thing can be the basis for genuine affirmation. Here are three simple ways to provide that genuine affirmation:

Compliment in private. Taking the time to note something that your boss did exceptionally well and then mentioning it to your boss privately is a great way for you to give qi (see the Introduction to Part 3, "Lead Your Peers," for a primer on qi giving versus qi sucking).* A simple affirmation will suffice: "Boss, it really inspired me when you stood up in front of the organization and delivered that tough message with such compassion and balance. Great job!" And if delivering a compliment in person is not an option or is awkward, a handwritten note can also get the message across.

Praise in public. Tell your boss's boss something you admire or respect about the person you work for. Find an opportunity to make your boss look good. Imagine if the people who work for you were committed to doing that for you!

Say thank you. Remember to be gracious and display good manners. When your boss does something thoughtful or kind or supportive, thank them. Reinforce that positive behavior with your gratitude and acknowledgment. I had one colleague who wouldn't even say thank you for the generous holiday gift he received because he was so angry with our boss. I found that not only immature but incredibly foolish. Why would you willfully

DELIVERING THE MESSAGE

If it's not possible to tell your boss in person, even sending a quick text message, email, or phone call will work. The point is to acknowledge them in a timely, sincere matter. Delivery method matters less than actually delivering the message.

---

* Here's the lowdown: qi (pronounced "chee") is energy, according to Eastern philosophies. Qi sucking occurs anytime you take more energy from a person or group during an interaction than you give. Qi giving is the opposite. Take a moment right now: I'm sure you can think of several chronic qi suckers in your workplace.

ignore a great opportunity to make a positive deposit in the relationship bank account?

These suggestions may seem simplistic, but they are incredibly powerful. There is nothing better than a well-timed, honest, positive statement of appreciation from another human being. This is truth telling. And it is doubly powerful when given to your boss. That's because most leaders hear nothing but complaints, and about problems and "issues," from the folks who work for them. It's not because their people don't appreciate them. It's just that getting into a rut of heads-down-bums-up-work-all-the-time is so easy. We don't stop to think that the boss might need a bit of encouragement from time to time, just like we do.

> **You need to challenge, push back, and tell your boss things they might not want to hear. That is true partnership.**

When you take a moment to give your boss the gift of authentic from-the-heart affirmation—no matter how flawed they are as a leader—you are not only doing the right thing, you are also demonstrating wisdom, humanity, and maturity.

But don't suck up. Don't polish the apple. Think about it: Would you want to be lied to by your direct reports for flattery's sake? Don't do that to your boss either. While the old adage "If you can't say anything nice, don't say anything at all" is true on one level, it is also true that you can rise above and look for opportunities and evidence where your leader does something well. And then acknowledge it.

If you truly want to be a person your boss believes in, trusts, relies on, and listens to (and wants to promote!), you need to challenge, push back, and tell your boss things they might not want to hear. That is true partnership.

If you want to kick, you'd better learn how to stroke.

18

And Now, the Kick

AHHHH. SO HERE we are. We've finally arrived at one of the big questions on how to effectively lead your boss. How can you challenge your leader—push back—without committing career suicide?

If you have faithfully applied over the long term the stroke part of the stroke, stroke, kick method described in Chapter 17, the "kick" you give your boss will likely be far more positively received. The key is to push back in a way that can be heard.

In the previous chapter, you read about the importance of finding authentic ways and moments in which to acknowledge and compliment your leader.

Here's the greatest benefit of doing that on a consistent basis: when you "kick" your boss by disagreeing vehemently, pushing back on an idea, or taking an opposing view, you will have a wellspring of goodwill that you can draw on.

For most people, being disagreed with is an unpleasant experience. We tend to prefer that others agree with us. Enthusiastically.

You will hear leaders say, "Tell me what you really think" or "Push back on me, I love a good debate" or other such nonsense. My experience is to be especially careful with these bosses, as the opposite tends to be true. That said, no matter whom you are working for or what their personality is, it is imperative that you speak up, challenge, and share your point of view. But do it in a manner in which and at a time when your leader can hear you and respond positively.

Therein lies the art of being courageous.

DISAGREEING AND BEING HEARD IS AN ART

MANY BUSINESS PROFESSIONALS blunder through the workplace loudly proclaiming their superiority for "telling it like it is" and not sugarcoating things. Those people also tend to not get promoted much.

One person in particular springs to mind. Throughout the company, he was known as the "Unabomber" because he had a terrible habit of dropping verbal bombs on superiors, peers, and team members whenever he had something to say.

No diplomacy. No sensitivity to timing. No promotion.

And guess what? He wanted advancement so badly, but he would scoff when told that it was his approach to disagreements and debates within the business that were holding him back. His response? "That's me. I tell it like it is. I say what everyone is thinking but no one else wants to say."

That colleague may have been correct in his point of view, but he had minimal positive impact because of how he approached disagreements. It is one thing to say to your boss what you think. It is an entirely different thing to actually be *heard*.

Being heard means being taken seriously. Your perspective is welcome. Valued. Worth considering. And although your leader may find it intellectually challenging to contemplate your point of view, they won't feel *emotionally* challenged hearing it. Why not? Because it is coming from you. And you have a positive track record. You consistently make your boss look good and, more importantly, *feel* good. (Remember, there needs to be a 2:1 ratio of strokes to kicks.)

> **Remember, there needs to be a 2:1 ratio of strokes to kicks.**

Humans like to be liked. Humans like to be appreciated. Humans like to be acknowledged. Humans like to receive sincere praise. Humans like to feel good.

You are human. And you like all that stuff.

So does your boss.

If you have been applying the techniques discussed in this book, if you have been doing all these positive things, it will be almost laughable how easy it will be to disagree with your leader and how unthreatening for them.

HOW TO TEE UP A DISAGREEMENT

THERE IS A simple way to let your boss know that you disagree with them. Tell them. Say:

> *"Boss, I need to disagree with you on this issue. May I tell you why?"*

(If you work for a nightmare leader the response might be a curt "No." If you suspect that will be the answer, don't ask "May I tell you why?")

Another, more humorous way to approach your boss—one I have used to great success—is to say:

"Boss, I know you have the 'glow stick of destiny,' so you can do whatever you want on this issue. I just need to tell you my thoughts, and then you do what you will with them."

And then tell your leader what your view is.

There is power in giving your boss a moment or two to prepare for the pushback that's coming. It's a small thing, but it can increase the odds of your being heard.

Or you might grab your leader after a meeting and say:

"I know you feel strongly about X issue and taking Y approach. I've been doing a lot of thinking about this and would like to schedule 15 minutes to share with you my perspective."

Or you might say:

"Boss, when we first started working together you told me you wanted me to push back, disagree with you, and share my thoughts. This is one of those times I need to take you up on that invitation."

See how this works?

You are preparing your leader to be disagreed with before you actually disagree. It's like tenderizing steak before you grill it.

An Easy Technique for Disagreeing Agreeably

Years ago, I learned a simple but powerful technique while attending the Walton Institute* as an emerging leader at

---

* Sam and Helen Walton started this leadership program for store managers and all other leaders to provide them with foundational development. Later in my career at Walmart, I had the privilege to lead the programming and teach the course.

Walmart. This technique, which enables disagreement without being disagreeable, is called the LCS method. It can be used for small issues or large issues. It's a framework for offering up your point of view in a nonthreatening manner.

"LCS" stands for:

Like*

Concern

Suggest

Here is an example. When my son was 11 years old, he was relentless in wanting to get a bird for a pet. He went on a months-long campaign, with visits to the pet store, plus lots of Internet searches to find parrot pictures and research bird species, the results of which he would share with me at length.

I was resistant. Frankly, I thought getting a bird was a terrible idea and had zero desire or inclination to fulfill my son's wish.

One day when he asked (for the millionth time) if we could get a bird—if there was any reason to hope I might change my mind—I remembered the LCS method and so said the following:

> Son, I really *like* your passion for animals and totally get why you think parrots are beautiful and why you like them. My *concern* is that we already have two dogs that you are inconsistent in caring for. My *suggestion* is that you show me, through your daily behavior and over a significant period of time, that you can feed, water, walk, and play with the dogs consistently, and then we will discuss adding another pet to the household.

Now, this is a simple example but the framework can be applied to any situation. I have used it countless times and it

---

* In practice, you can insert any appropriate positive word or phrase.

works every time. Here are two important things to keep in mind when you use it with your leader:

1. It is important to identify something you genuinely agree with. You must start out with something you genuinely like about the point of view of your boss. If there is absolutely nothing you agree with, then at least appreciate the passion. Say something like, "Boss, I really respect and appreciate how passionate you are about this topic."

2. Wise positioning increases the likelihood of a positive reception. Be crisp and clear on where your disagreement lies but position it as your "concern" and then "suggestion." Both terms soften what you're saying and allow your listener to process more productively what you are conveying. Some leaders can take blunt language but most can't. Err on the side of caution.

DIPLOMACY IS WISER THAN BLUNTNESS

VERY FEW COMPANY cultures allow or encourage direct and challenging feedback. Paying lip service to the concept doesn't mean it is truly encouraged. And even when it is, it tends to be a one-way street from manager to underling. Sometimes peer to peer. Rarely upward. But in order for you to lead your boss and have a fulfilling work life by sharing your thoughts and ideas, and by contributing fully to the business, you must do it anyway.

No matter how direct your leader's communication style, remember that just because they can dish it doesn't mean they can take it. In fact, one of the critical things I learned when I became a Birkman Certified Consultant early in my career was that most people need a high degree of diplomacy in communication.* Specifically, they need a far greater degree of softness and sensitivity in the verbal communication they receive than they employ in their directness with others.

Did you catch the implication of that?

No matter how blunt your boss is in communicating with you, do not assume they can take that degree of directness back from you.

THE STOKE, STROKE, kick method is an important one to keep in mind for all the important relationships in your life. There is a relevant concept in the wisdom literature: "Speak the truth *in love*." "Love" is the most essential principle. It is only loving to share a "stroke" if it is genuine (i.e., the truth). It is only loving to "kick" if the truth, as you see it, is delivered in a manner that is digestible by the recipient. Using the LCS method to disagree is an easy way to ensure your perspective is communicated in a constructive manner.

> No matter how blunt your boss is in communicating with you, do not assume they can take that degree of directness back from you.

It is very difficult to find true fulfillment in your professional life if you are constantly biting your tongue, playing politics, and not sharing your ideas and perspective. You spend far too much time on the job not to bring your whole self to work every day and contribute.

---

* The Birkman Method is a personality, social perception, and occupational interest assessment used to identify behavioral styles, expectations, and stress behaviors. Corporate human resources professionals, educational institutions, and independent consultants have used the Birkman Method for more than 50 years and with over 2.5 million people. I absolutely love this tool!

You may employ all the techniques shared in this chapter and still have your ideas shut down or overruled. That's okay. That's a far better outcome than suppressing or just going along with things. You are draining your energy when you do that.

Enjoy pushing back on your leader. Just make sure you do it in a way that ensures they can *hear* you.

19

Putting It All Together: Leading Your Boss

THE INFORMATION IN this section of the book might have seemed elementary to you at times. You might have been scoffing and thinking, "Well, duh. I know that."

It's not the *knowing* that is the big deal. It's the actual *doing*.

And while the techniques described here are pretty basic and something most business professionals already know, it is quite rare that these techniques are actually put into practice.

Transformation and change is an inside-out job. You have to be willing to approach and engage with your leader differently. With a different mindset. With a different attitude. With a different intent. Then, what comes out of your mouth and how you follow that up with your actions will yield far different results.

If you truly can't have a different mindset or intent toward your boss—and you may have very good reasons for that—you need to get a new boss. And that's okay. People join companies and leave managers. Every day. Everywhere. There is no shame in that.

However, if there is a glimmer of hope regarding your boss, try to apply these techniques first. At the least you will have good practice in how you will start with your next boss. And on the upside, you may actually see positive change in your existing relationship such that it does not require you to change jobs or companies.

Here's a quick recap:

- Intensely study your leader to get to know the human being behind the mask. Seek out people who have worked with or for this person for long enough to have a credible view on who they are and how they operate. Ask your new boss probing questions. Be curious. Do your homework. This will save you an immense amount of time and pain later. (Chapter 12)

- Understand the company you work for, the business you are in, how the firm makes money, who the end customer is, and how what you do every day fits into the strategy of the company. You also need to understand the culture and how things really get done. This is table stakes. (Chapter 13)

- Get the boss-employee relationship basics right. Keep your leader informed and never surprise them. When you or your team makes a mistake, 'fess up and move forward with a plan to fix it. And give your boss the benefit of the doubt. (Chapter 14)

- Make a concerted effort to elevate your thinking to an enterprise-wide perspective. Frame your suggestions and solutions to business issues from this context and your ideas will be smarter and far more likely to be implemented. (Chapter 15)

- Get in tune with your leader by knowing exactly what they are wrestling with on a weekly basis. Ask what their single greatest priority for the upcoming week is, and then strive to bring them solutions to that issue. (Chapter 16)

- Provide honest, positive praise and affirmation to your boss— to them directly, and to their superiors and others. Look for traits that you admire or respect and communicate that. Always be truthful. Be deliberate and diligent about making deposits in your relationship bank account. (Chapter 17)

- Be smart by preparing your boss for your pushback, challenges, and disagreements. Use the LCS method to frame your differences so that your leader can *hear* what you have to say and positively respond. Don't suppress your views or just go along with things for political reasons. Tell the truth—just do it wisely. (Chapter 18)

PART
3

Lead Your Peers

ABOUT
"LEAD YOUR PEERS"

REALLY DEBATED WHETHER or not to write this section of the book. So much of what I planned to write seemed so obvious. But as I reflected on my career and the careers of my friends and colleagues, one area that didn't get much air time, yet caused so much tension on the job, was peer-to-peer relationships.

Early in my time at Walmart, I had a colleague named Amber. She and I had similar roles, but we served different employee populations. From the moment I landed in Bentonville, Arkansas, we were in constant competition. While I respected her experience, I never really liked her. I was guarded around her and suspicious of her motives.

I can't recall why I felt so strongly about her or what led to our competitive behavior. I just remember feeling drained by the relationship (such as it was) and believing that it was "either her or me"—that there wasn't space for us both to be successful. Which is a ridiculous notion when you consider that Walmart was the largest company in the world!

But peer relationships can roll like that. They are not necessarily rational. Looking back on that experience, I see that my beliefs about success in business were very confining.

I can contrast that to a significant moment I shared with Stewart, a friend and colleague, as we walked down the hall toward the office of Joe, one of our peers. The three of us worked for a particularly challenging boss, and he had been a beast to Joe that day. As Stewart and I talked about it, we agreed that we should speak with Joe. Stewart and I supported each other when the boss gave one of us a hard time, but we weren't sure Joe had anyone to talk to.

The conversation (and breakthrough) that occurred in the ensuing discussion was a turning point for all three of us. When we poked our heads into Joe's office and said we were coming to give moral support—because we knew how much it sucked to get the "you-can't-do-anything-right-you-must-be-stupid" lecture from our boss—Joe was astounded.

He shared with us how alone he always felt at work, and how he thought he was the only one who felt that way. He had no idea that we did too and was so thankful that we had reached out. From that one conversation, the relationships among the three of us immediately improved and deepened.

So many themes jump out of that story for me. "Treat others the way you would want to be treated" comes to mind as one very important one. But beyond that is the truth mentioned many times throughout this book: the only thing you can reliably control or change at your company is yourself. You will find many permutations of this philosophy in the chapters that follow. For instance, one way I like to think about engaging with peers and colleagues (and all people, actually) is to ask myself after every interaction whether I was a qi giver or a qi sucker.

Qi (pronounced "chee"), according to Eastern philosophy, is energy, both physical and metaphysical. So qi sucking is simply taking more energy from an exchange with another human being than you give.

I want to help you be a qi giver with all of your colleagues and customers, but especially with your peers. Those relationships can make or break your daily experience. The principles and tips provided, while appearing simple on the surface, can drive tremendous positive change in your work life because, at their essence, they are qi givers.

Here is what you'll find in this section:

Chapter 20 encourages you to *fall in like* with your colleagues by inviting them to your home for a meal.

Chapter 21 explores collaboration across functional and business boundaries, and how to demonstrate it yourself.

Chapter 22 focuses on truth telling and having the courage to resolve a conflict with a peer as soon as it arises.

Chapter 23 explores the art of apologizing.

Chapter 24 delves into the idea of asking and offering help, often and proactively.

Chapter 25 looks at the importance of praising your colleagues to the boss and others.

Chapter 26 pulls it all together into a concise recap.

Being part of a great team in which you have rock-solid relationships makes all the tough times—generated by annoying bosses or difficult direct reports—so much easier. And it's just more fun to adore the peers you work with.

In each of the chapters in this part—whether focused on cross-functional teaming, giving a great apology, or addressing a conflict head-on—you find qi-giving tools and techniques to help you build super-healthy, connected relationships with your peers.

So let's get the qi flowing!

20

Falling in Like—The Best Office Romance

WHEN I LIVED in New Jersey while working at the global headquarters of Campbell Soup Company, I instituted a Saturday morning tradition that my toddler son and I adored. We had a pancake brunch every weekend. I would make pancakes from scratch, plus scrambled eggs and bacon and all the fixings. We had a blast cooking together.

When I mentioned this to colleagues at work, a few of them moaned appreciatively and said how long it had been since they'd had homemade pancakes, and how much they loved them. I immediately encouraged them to come over the following weekend. I assured them that I would be cooking whether they were there or not, so they might as well come on over and enjoy pancakes with me and my son.

Many took me up on that invitation. The word spread, and over the several years we lived there, many coworkers and their families showed up for those Saturday morning brunches. It was great fun.

But for me, it wasn't just fun. It was also a great way to get to know my colleagues. To see them outside the office, interacting with their families. To put a human face on the serious professionals I worked with during the week. And they got to do the same with me.

It humanized all of us and it helped me *fall in like* with them.

We all click with certain colleagues at work, and those relationships seem effortless from the beginning. But with other people it can be hard. When we disagree or things aren't going well, it can take a tremendous amount of effort and energy to be productive and professional.

> **Pick the people you really struggle to like and invite them to your home. They will be shocked by the invitation, and you will be surprised by how fun they and their families really are.**

When we like someone, though, it's a million times easier. And there is no better accelerator to falling in like with your colleagues than to invite them into your home to share a meal. It may sound a bit old-fashioned, and it's something that's rarely done anymore, but it's a tradition worth reviving.

If you truly want to get to know who's who in the zoo, invite your peers over for dinner (or a pancake brunch). The majority of the time, you'll be delighted by the result—and by the positive impact it has on your work.

WHAT TO DO

SO, WHAT'S THE best way to tackle this method of getting to know your peers better and building better relationships with them? Plan to have every colleague and their family over to your home in the next year. Then schedule it in.

Share with your significant other why this is important to you and explain how they can help.

Here are three quick tips to help you on your way:

1. Pick the people you really struggle to like or get to know and invite them first. They will be shocked by the invitation, and you will be surprised by how fun (or how weird!) they and their families really are.

2. Invite international or out-of-state colleagues over to your home for dinner when they travel to your work location. For them, a homemade meal will be *so* much better than one more restaurant meal; for you, it's a great way to build bridges with peers you don't see every day.

3. Keep it simple. If you hate to cook, buy prepared food at the grocery store or order in pizza or Chinese. The experience will be mutually enjoyable only if you yourself are relaxed and able to focus on getting to know your colleague.

I have found that it's better to do these in-home dinners with one peer and their family, as opposed to having a couple of peers and their families over at the same time. The purpose is relationship building and getting to know your colleague, their spouse, and their family. Be curious about who they are beyond work and where they've come from. With a bigger group, the dynamics change and relationship building is more difficult.

I often use TableTopics cards, cards printed with questions designed to start great conversations. There are all sorts of editions. My favorite is Not Your Mom's Dinner Party Table Topics. There are various ways to employ these little babies—one easy way is to tuck a couple of cards under each plate and then at some point during the meal have everyone pull theirs out and answer the questions round-robin style.

It's fun and the answers are usually spontaneous—and get both hilarious and meaningful conversations flowing. Don't worry about it feeling contrived. Believe me—I've done this countless times, and people are always grateful for provocative, fun topics to talk about. Besides, great conversations are a rarity these days!

DOES DINING AT A RESTAURANT COUNT?

I CAN ALREADY hear the excuses: "Oh, Mindy, I can't have people from work over to my house! My house is too small (or messy, or a disaster, etc.). Plus, my kids are a nightmare. Besides, I can't cook—I'm just too busy."

DON'T BE AFRAID TO DELEGATE

As all my friends and colleagues know, I am a huge fan of games at parties—whether I'm entertaining 80 parents from my son's class at school or having another family over for a casual dinner. Novelty, spontaneity, and a sense of humor are your best friends. You introverts are probably cringing and thinking, "Mindy, are you kidding me? It's hard enough to envision just inviting these strangers into my home, let alone playing some type of game. I can think of nothing worse, actually!" Don't worry, you are not alone: if you are an introvert, you may have an extrovert as a partner (it's a common pairing), so go ahead and delegate the game or conversation starter to them. Or to one of your children, if you have kids and they're old enough. It doesn't have to be all on you. Relax. Just keep the wine glasses filled and participate. The point is to do something fun and different—the evening is sure to be memorable and provide lots of laughs for you and your colleague.

Come on, people! There is nothing nicer than being invited over to someone's house and having a good chat over some food and wine. No one cares anymore about whether the food was cooked or bought prepared from the grocery store. People are just thrilled to be getting together...in someone's home no less! This is true for the friends in your life, and it's doubly true for your peers at work.

Before you dismiss this idea entirely and instead grudgingly say you'll meet your colleague at a restaurant, let me share with you why I believe going to a restaurant is suboptimal:

- It's not truly a gift of hospitality you are offering, even if you pick up the check. And with a colleague, even with spouses present, it will feel like just one more business dinner.

- You are able to maintain a reserve and emotional distance more easily. No vulnerability is required. Hosting someone in your home, however, even if you are just having pizza, beer, and a game of cards, has a far higher impact because you are in your natural environment and revealing something of your life.

You may find yourself resisting this concept. The resistance likely has to do with some inadequacy you feel about yourself, your life, or your home—the very things that make you human. Revealing your humanity in this manner is a form of vulnerability because you can't control everything your kids or spouse will do or say, or any mishap that may occur.

That's the fun part, because there is nothing more real than having a colleague see you and your family interact in your natural environment, embarrassing as it may be. It lowers the barriers between you and your peer and accelerates relationship building, never mind providing an entertaining shared experience.

BOTTOM LINE? BE relaxed, hospitable, and curious, and have some fun. There will be a definite positive shift in your peer relationship from that point forward, and you will find that working through tough issues at work becomes markedly easier.

Go ahead—it's time for you to *fall in like* with your colleagues!

21

The Power of
Cross-Functional Teaming

THE MARCH 2015 edition of *Harvard Business Review* included an article titled "Why Strategy Execution Unravels—And What to Do about It." The authors point out that most leaders believed that what interfered with executing a strategy was not their own team but their peers' teams. In essence, leaders believed that their teams were fine—it was everyone else who caused the problems.

Given leaders' penchant for blaming the other guy, it should come as no surprise that those leaders were ineffective at resolving conflict with peers. Maybe assigning blame is just human nature. Either way, it's dangerous and counterproductive.

When I first arrived at Jim Beam, my HR team would talk about how difficult it was to work with the finance team. Remedying this wasn't a huge priority for me, until one day I was deliberately fed incomplete numbers by a mid-level finance manager who was also unwilling to cough up all the information I had requested.

I was pretty ticked off and marched down to the office of the CFO to have a discussion with him. I was planning on calling the finance manager into my office for a "come to Jesus," but I wasn't going to do it without talking to my peer first.

As Bob, the CFO, and I discussed what had happened, we began to talk about how our teams weren't working together very well. There was a history of mistrust and disrespect between Finance and HR. Neither group was acting maturely and each was quick to blame the other team when things went awry. Bob had arrived a year before me and was in the middle of a turnaround within his function. I was just at the beginning with mine.

We agreed to present a united front. We would speak to our respective leadership teams and tell them that a new era of cooperation and trust was beginning, and that we would not tolerate any gamesmanship.

I called in Bob's finance manager to give him some feedback on his little stunt with the numbers; Bob had done the same. So the message that we were aligned and meant what we said got around fast.

SET THE EXPECTATION

IT IS IMPOSSIBLE to meet expectations on the job without healthy relationships across departments and functions. And it is up to you as a leader to set that expectation by doing two things:

1. Tell your team that you expect every member to behave honorably and collaboratively with their peers in other functions, and that territorialism and passive-aggressive behavior won't

be tolerated. Expect them to treat their colleagues in the same manner they want to be treated.

2. Demonstrate all of this yourself. Every day. And you must do so with your peers who lead the other functions and business units.

As with anything, saying it is one thing—doing it is another.

LEAD WITH LUNCH

A GREAT WAY for you to show solidarity with your peers is to go out to lunch with them individually every few months.

When people in an organization see their leaders chatting away as they head out the door to grab a bite to eat, it increases their confidence. It shows that relationships are important and worth investing time in. It also shows that a foundation is being built, so that even when there are disagreements (and there always are), there is an underpinning healthy relationship.

If you have peers in other geographies, make a point of scheduling one-on-one time—coffee or a meal—with them when you are visiting their market. Don't just wing in for two or three days of meetings and then leave town.

Force yourself to do this with the peers on the team you find difficult to connect with. At first, it won't be as much fun as your lunches with the peers you naturally get along with. But it's essential for breaking down barriers and forging a mutually respectful relationship.

AFTER SEVERAL YEARS, the collaboration and solid relationship between the HR and Finance functions at Jim Beam were so notable that Bob and I were invited to jointly present at a CFO conference in Chicago. Our topic was teaching leaders to positively transform the relationship between these two critical functions.

Even better, Bob and I had become best friends at work—which, given how I marched into his office that snowy day early on in my tenure, speaks to his relaxed temperament!

22

Telling the Whole Truth—And Nothing but the Truth

YOU NEED TO start telling the truth to your peers. The whole truth. And nothing but the truth.

I can hear you right now.

"You can't be serious, Mindy. Tell the truth? The whole truth? At work? To whom, exactly? And about what, precisely? Are you trying to get me fired?"

No, I'm not encouraging you to self-immolate on the job.

I am encouraging you to *care enough to call it* when something at work is broken. When there is tension in a peer relationship. When there is something simmering under the surface. Or simmering right out in the open. Over and over, I have seen the damage wrought by people avoiding addressing an issue with a coworker.

As a chief human resources officer, one of my inviolate rules was: I will not listen to griping about a peer by a member of the leadership team who hasn't tried to deal with the issue directly with the colleague.

The first time I cut off a member of the executive team mid-rant about a colleague, the ranter was astonished. For some time, that team had been seen throughout the organization as highly dysfunctional. The board knew it. The senior leaders knew it. In fact, the guys in the mailroom knew it. The executive team was embarrassing itself, and its relationship squabbles were a total waste of time and focus. But it sure gave everyone a lot to gossip about.

Our new CEO was committed to repairing this craziness. He communicated that to me when he hired me shortly after his arrival.

Not long after that, there I was, interrupting a rant by saying politely but firmly that I wasn't interested. I was happy to help anyone who had talked to their peer about whatever the problem was. But otherwise I needed to get back to work.

The executive stormed out of my office, saying I wasn't doing my job as an HR leader.

I disagreed.

Conflict aversion and avoidance is at epidemic proportions in businesses today. I have observed time and again how smart, capable, well-intentioned business leaders dance around their handbags with other colleagues because they don't want to address an issue head-on. The issue just lingers and lingers. And gets bigger and bigger. Sometimes the issue reaches epic proportion and requires someone to leave the organization.

> **You'll know you need to deal with the situation when you hear yourself venting about a peer. That's your big clue.**

What a waste!

A great example of conflict avoidance involves a friend of mine who is a senior executive at a large global company. She got super pissed off at one of her peers. She knew her colleagues shared in her frustration—she'd heard them kvetch about the guy for a long time. But while they all complained, no one had the courage to deal with the issue directly because the person was a nightmare to deal with.

When my friend experienced firsthand what her peers had been talking about, she was not happy. Not one bit. But instead of doing what her colleagues had done, she scheduled a meeting with her peer, sat down, and very calmly said to him, "I am really pissed off right now. I felt incredibly disrespected when you did X. It will be extremely difficult for us to have a good working relationship if you do that again."

The guy was absolutely stunned by her candor. And then manned up and apologized.

And he never did it again. At least not to my friend.

Pretty incredible, right?

Imagine how good you would feel if you simply dealt with an uncomfortable issue head-on in a calm, measured way—and especially if you got the issue resolved once and for all. No more tension. It would be a tremendous relief, wouldn't it?

You'll know you need to deal with the situation when you hear yourself venting about a peer. That's your big clue.

I'm not saying it will be comfortable. But if you truly care about the organization and about having healthy, constructive relationships, you will have the courage to step up and have the conversation.

Here are three tips on how to do it effectively:

1. Plan what you will say. Don't go off half-cocked!

2. Schedule a time specifically to address the issue, and make sure you are rested and aren't feeling rushed.

3. Share with the person your sincere desire to resolve the issue and tell them that you are dealing with them directly about this issue because you do not want things to fester and to get in the way of a good working relationship—even if it means feeling uncomfortable at the moment.

You can't control the other person's reaction. You can't change what they've done or will choose to do in the future. All you can do is go to your colleague and tell them the truth about what they've done and how you feel. Give your colleague the opportunity to fix it.

Relationships really are a two-way street. On your side of the street, courageously addressing issues with your coworkers is your responsibility.

Forgive the use of an old cliché, but relationships really are a two-way street. On your side of the street, courageously addressing issues with your coworkers is your responsibility.

It's time for you to tell your colleagues the truth—the *whole* truth.

23

Saying You're Sorry

A S YOU'RE BUSY telling the *whole* truth to your colleague, you may discover that their response is to bring up a mistake you have made.

Gulp.

Throughout my career I have worked for Canadian, British, and Australian—along with a host of American—bosses, and all three of them have used the term "prat" liberally to describe when someone is being an idiot. And in this case, the term fits.

It's time to stop being a prat and apologize.

You would think, based on the frequency of sincere apologies that occur in the corporate world today, that every business professional were approaching sainthood. When I ask audiences at my keynotes when was the last time they received an apology from a coworker, it becomes obvious that it is rarely a recent or even semi-recent event. But if I ask about the last time someone at work was a complete bonehead and messed up... well, it was, like, just five minutes ago!

Ah, human nature is such a lovely, beastly thing.

I won't go on a qi-sucking soliloquy here. Suffice to say that you are a qi sucker at work at times. I know this because you are a human being. Remember, in Eastern philosophies, *qi* refers to physical and metaphysical energy. So qi sucking is taking more energy than you give during an exchange with another person or group of people.

We all know habitual qi suckers. These are the folks we duck and run from as soon as we see them coming. I hope you are not a chronic qi sucker. Unfortunately, chronic qi suckers rarely self-identify. So if you are one, you are likely completely unaware of your qi-sucking behaviors.

But the rest of you *do* know when you've messed up or missed the mark. You *do* have that twinge of guilt or regret for being a prat, even while giving yourself a pass because you didn't intend to be one.*

Unfortunately, the ultimate qi-suck is to make a mistake or do something thoughtless, and then not apologize for it. And

---

LEAD BY EXAMPLE
. . . .

Leading your peers requires you to lead by example. One incredibly important way to do that is to 'fess up when you mess up. It's simple. It's basic. But it is game-changing. It's hard to have credibility if you don't operate in this way.

---

* This is where the fancy social psychology term "fundamental attribution error" comes in. Basically, it refers to our judging our fine selves by our *intent* (I didn't *intend* to lose my temper and call that guy a jerk, it just happened because I'm stressed out and have a lot on my mind. Ooops!), while judging harshly others based on their *impact* (I cannot bee-leeve that a-hole called me a jerk!) and ascribe their lousy behavior to their character.

because it has been *sooooo* long since any of you have likely made an apology, I'm going to remind you what a great apology looks and sounds like.

THE THREE ELEMENTS OF A GREAT APOLOGY

1. Actually saying "I'm sorry" out loud—while making eye contact, if possible.
2. Acknowledging your error by adding the phrase "I was wrong . . . but more importantly, you were right." (This is my brother's favorite part of the apology—especially when he's on the receiving end. Add the second part only if that is in fact the case.)
3. Asking humbly, "How can I fix this?" Keep in mind that an effective apology requires you to have actually begun working on a solution by the time you get to this step.

Apologizing well is such an important skill, I think you should stop reading and practice doing it right now.

I'm not kidding.

[Big pause while you do this.]

This is one of the favorite parts of my keynotes to an audience of business professionals. They laugh a lot and then try it. By the second or third time, they really get into it.

After practicing these three phrases, one man cracked me up when he said, "I need to go home right away and apologize to my wife. It will take me days to make up for all the years I haven't apologized."

Yes, sir, go home right now and apologize to your poor wife!

SEVERAL YEARS AGO I was on a routine market visit with a sales team in Idaho. We'd stopped for a quick bite to eat. The conversation over lunch centered on the business, and these long-tenured sales guys, including the sales leader, were regaling me with their frustrations about a particular group at Home Office. It was the marketing group, including its GM.

The complaining went something like this:

> *"They never get the pricing strategy right. We can't make our volume numbers with the price increases they want us to put in on this brand!"*

> *"I hate the latest brand campaign. It was better in the old days when sales controlled all the marketing and we could do what was right for our market."*

> *(And the clincher:) "This GM doesn't have a clue how the business works!"*

"Do you honestly believe," I asked them, "that this GM and her team wake up every day and say to themselves, 'How can we make life supremely difficult for the Idaho team—and, in fact, how can we impede their ability to sell this brand we are all accountable for? That's our goal!'?"

All three guys stopped speaking, looked at me, and then started laughing.

Ironically, not long before my visit to Idaho, I had had a similar conversation—about getting better connected with the sales team—with the very GM they were referencing.

My recommendation was the same for each group. Pick up the phone, start building the relationship, and get together. Walk the proverbial mile and try to understand *why* those in the other group have taken a certain position—instead of assuming they are morons.

The sales guys didn't know or trust the GM. The GM didn't know or trust the sales guys. Everyone was busy. Each person had an excuse for not reaching out first and instead blaming the other guy.

The sales leader took our conversation to heart. He picked up the phone and invited the GM to come into the market and spend the day on the ground with the customers and his team so that he could pick her brain on the brand plans.

That day was an eye-opener for both of them. The GM became far more informed about what was frustrating the sales team. And the sales guys had a much clearer view of the rationale for the national brand strategy.

The kicker in all of this, though, was what the GM told me a few weeks later. She shared with me how she was dumbfounded when, at the end of the day, the sales leader—this big, burly sales dude who'd been in the booze business all his life—apologized for being so difficult and resistant and not reaching out sooner. She couldn't believe it!

Never in her career, as far she knew, had a sales colleague apologized to a marketing colleague. (Unfortunately, in the consumer packaged-goods industry, that *is* a rare occurrence.)

You can guess the rest of the story. From then on, both groups worked together far more productively and proactively.

All because of a simple, sincere apology.

There is nothing quite so powerful.

And it is a skill that can truly never be overused.

Imagine how stunning it would be if one of your colleagues came up to you, pulled you aside, and said, "Listen, I screwed up.

I'm really sorry. I was wrong when I [fill in the blank]. But more importantly, you were right, and here's how I'm going to fix it."

Why does this feel so good? Because despite the mistake the person made, their acknowledgment of the mistake is an energy boost for you. They just gave you a serious qi deposit!

Your goal is to not be a qi sucker. But when you do miss the mark and make a mistake, you can repair and regain trust by the ultimate "qi give"—the apology.

Remember, everyone is doing the best they can. Each day you wake up and have the positive intent to be a good person, do a good job, and make a difference. That is the natural state of most people. Even when you are in a bad mood, or things are crazy at work, or you have massive stress in your life, your general intent is to be a decent human being.

Failing to apologize for missing the mark, making a mistake, or generally being an idiot is the ultimate qi-suck.

That's also true for every one of your colleagues.

Gang, we all know that to err is human. But failing to apologize for missing the mark, making a mistake, or generally being an idiot is the ultimate qi-suck.

Don't suck qi.

Don't be a prat.

Start giving great apologies instead.

24

Positive Relationships
Made Easy

D R. BRENÉ BROWN is widely recognized as one of the leading experts on a subject many people can relate to: vulnerability. With her now-famous TED Talk "The Power of Vulnerability" and her subsequent appearances on Oprah Winfrey's show, along with her numerous bestsellers, Brown has influenced both the personal development and business genres.

Attending one of her speeches, I was deeply impressed by how she described vulnerability as a combination of uncertainty, risk, and emotional exposure. This description perfectly captures what is involved in lowering your guard and asking for help. An act of vulnerability, yes, but also an act of courage.

I wasn't thinking about courage or vulnerability when I took the initiative to learn how to drive an 18-wheeler during my first year at Walmart. I was thinking about survival. This was my first "real" business job after my years at graduate school, where I got my master's in marriage and family therapy. Not only did I know nothing about HR, I also knew nothing about logistics and transportation. Yet that was the division in which I found myself after I was hired as a personnel manager.

I believed that the only way I would ever get my "clients"—the employees I served—to reach out to me for support was by thoroughly understanding their work life. That included how they did their jobs. And that's how I ended up learning how to drive tractor-trailers, do preventive maintenance, cube a trailer on the dock, and drop loads in the distribution-center yard.

Learning all that required my asking for help from guys who had been doing these jobs for years. But that was how I could learn about their typical day. I knew that doing this would help me be more compassionate, and hopefully smarter, when making judgment calls.

I discovered early on that everyone was happy to help me learn. They were not annoyed, as I initially feared they might be. They were generous with their time and knowledge, and pleasantly surprised by my curiosity and desire to learn—no one in management had ever shown this level of interest before.

This has proved the case throughout my career. I learned early that the best way to round out my knowledge is to ask questions when I don't know the answers. And to avoid acting as if I am the supreme guru on all topics, when in reality I might not have a clue.

I'll never forget one conversation I had with a senior leader, who was shocked that I had gone to our CFO and asked for a primer on the balance sheet. He said, "I would be too embarrassed to go ask—because he would know I didn't know, and I'm supposed to know that stuff!"

That's a typical fear but also misguided. This particular leader was a brilliant sales executive. He had deep knowledge about a lot of important areas of the business. Just like the CFO had a great body of useful knowledge about other areas. But neither knew everything the other did, and they both would have benefited from being far more humble so that they could learn from the other rather than keeping up a façade.

HOW TO BUILD GREAT RELATIONSHIPS

HERE ARE FOUR ways to build meaningful, authentic relationships with your peers:

1. *Seek out their help in areas where you are weak and they are strong.* Yes, that requires you to lower your guard and admit you don't know everything about everything. It requires vulnerability. But it yields great results. You are increasing your knowledge and also paying a huge compliment to the person by acknowledging and valuing their expertise.

> Just acknowledging that you are aware of the pressure that one of your peers is facing is both a show of humanity and a way to make a large deposit in your mutual relationship's bank account.

2. *Invite them to speak at a team meeting you are conducting.* Let them share their knowledge and answer questions. It's about mutual respect.

3. *Proactively offer your help and support.* This is the flip side of inviting peers to speak at your meeting. Several years ago, I was involved in a delicate situation with one of my company's international leaders. It ultimately required flying halfway around the world to have a series of very difficult conversations on behalf of the company. Only a handful of

executives on our team were aware of the situation. To a person, they all individually took me aside and said, "Mindy, if there is anything I can do to help out or support you, please let me know. I am here for you. Call anytime." Those offers of help meant the world to me. I needed their support and was grateful to have such amazingly generous and kind colleagues.

4. *Look for opportunities with your peers to provide ideas and encouragement, a pair of hands, or a listening ear.* Just acknowledging that you are aware of the pressure that one of your peers is facing is both a show of humanity and a way to make a large deposit in your mutual relationship's bank account.

Your Turn to *Ask*
Take a moment to identify a few areas that you need to learn more about in the business and which of your peers is the expert:

AREA	EXPERT PEER

Prioritize reaching out to these peers—ideally in person—and let them know that you are intentionally trying to get smarter about the business and would love to get 15 minutes (or however long you think you need) of their time to ask questions and have them share their expertise on a certain topic. I guarantee they will be both flattered and happy to help you out.

Your Turn to *Offer*

Now think about each of your peers for a moment and what they are currently working on. Who is particularly burdened? Are they and their team intensely stressed? Capture their names and projects here:

PEER	GNARLY PROJECT/STRESSOR

Make a point today and over the coming days to drop in on these folks to say the following:

> *"[Insert peer's name here], I just wanted to drop by to see if there was anything my team or I could do to help out. I know you are under a ton of pressure due to [Name gnarly project/ stressor]. How can I help?"*

You know the response you will get. Your colleague will be amazed at and grateful for your thoughtfulness. *And* you just might be able to help them out, which is even better.

STRONG RELATIONSHIPS ARE built on positive interactions like the ones described above. Making the effort to both ask for help and offer support are qi-giving behaviors that will increase goodwill between you and your colleagues. Role model this consistently and you will find that you are surrounded by active, enthusiastic support when you need it most.

And when it comes to courageously addressing uncomfortable topics at work, you will be able to do so with far more confidence in a positive outcome.

25

Praise, Praise, Praise

WHEN I WAS on the executive team at Jim Beam, as the senior vice president and chief performance officer of the company (a fancy-schmancy title for running strategy and human resources globally), we brought in a terrific consulting firm that specializes in assessing senior leaders and providing subsequent development and coaching.*

Following an in-depth talent assessment of each of us on the executive team, we gave time at one of our quarterly strategy meetings to reviewing the results and sharing which areas were identified as needing personal development. Everyone had a chance to provide additional feedback and reiterate the areas each of us should work on.

One of my colleagues, Bryan, who was quite reserved, was given well-earned recognition. As we went around the room,

---

* Dr. Paul Eccher, the founder of The Vaya Group, worked with us for many years. He is not only a dear friend now but an incredibly insightful and challenging partner who has given me a ton of valuable (though not always pleasant) feedback throughout my career. Let me thank you here, Paul, for never letting me bamboozle you!

everyone adding their perspective, only positive things were said about Bryan: He was a joy to work with. His willingness to collaborate was much appreciated. His ego never got in the way. Not one person had anything negative to say about him, yet he had provided a list of areas in which he believed he needed to improve.

This was an awesome team moment. It was so gratifying to see someone so humble receive acknowledgment and encouragement from the entire group.

Bryan was amazing in an area that's a surefire driver of terrific peer relationships: he actively looked for ways to make others look good. If he was praised for something, he would give credit to his team. If he was working with a colleague, he praised his peer to the boss and downplayed his own participation.

And he was absolutely sincere. The guy was genuinely and consistently humble, and an example to the rest of us on the team. He was actually so taken aback by all the positive comments from the team that he asked me later if I had put them up to it. I just laughed and told him I didn't possess that kind of magical HR fairy dust.

WHY PRAISING OTHERS MAKES YOU LOOK GOOD

BEING ABLE TO credit others' talents and contributions is an important skill to develop. It is a powerful way to express support of those you work with, and it sets a great example to others in the organization. Try these three simple actions:

Challenge yourself to look for ways to highlight the good work and talents of your peers in front of your boss. Just as those you lead need to know you support them, your peers too need to know you support them. Finding ways to do that deserves your conscious attention.

Share the credit. There is plenty of it to go around, even if it doesn't feel like it at times. There is talk in the positive psychology movement about an abundance mindset versus a scarcity mindset. Any time you operate with the former, you tend to attract positive experiences—like receiving praise and credit from colleagues. On the other hand, when you believe there is a *limited supply* of whatever good stuff you desire, you are operating from a scarcity mindset. If you withhold sharing credit and praise with your peers, you will be far less likely to receive an abundance of it from them.

Compliment your colleagues to their faces. Tell them how they have impressed you or why you respect them. This is a major emotional-bucket filler (Stephen Covey is credited with popularizing the concept of the emotional bank account—I love this metaphor!). It should not have been a surprise to Bryan during our team meeting that his peers thought so highly of him. If we had all been telling him that directly along the way, he wouldn't have been so taken aback.

> Just as those you lead need to know you support them, your peers too need to know you support them.

When you consistently practice these three actions, you will notice how much more you are admired and respected by your colleagues. Sincerely role modeling these behaviors tends to beget more of the same from those you work with. Bottom line? It makes you look good.

YOU GOTTA WANT TO

SOME OF THE most rewarding feedback we received as an executive team came after the close of the sale of our company—liquor giant Jim Beam—to Japan's Suntory Holdings. At the deal dinner hosted by our investment bankers and law-firm partners, these professionals said they'd never worked with a more respectful group of executives. Specifically, they recounted how complimentary we all were about our colleagues—and (unfortunately) how unusual that was.

We appreciated the feedback. But for the most part we weren't surprised because that's how we always were with one another. We *did* respect our colleagues' talents. It's not that we were unaware of shortcomings, but we had such strong relationships based on mutual trust and respect that our various crazy traits weren't relevant.

This may seem a tad optimistic to you if you're on a team with folks you don't particularly like. You are not alone. I didn't necessarily like every member of the team either every single minute of every day.

You can make the choice, however, to look for the aspects of your peers that you respect. Their experience. Their knowledge. Their individual approach. If you want to find something to admire, you will find it. But you gotta want to. (And don't forget my earlier advice about how to accelerate *falling in like* with your colleagues—it really does work.)

Willingness to share evidence of that strength with others, especially the boss, is an incredible demonstration of leading your peers. It's treating them how you would want to be treated.

26

Putting It All Together: Leading Your Peers

ONE TEAM, ONE dream.

I have often used that phrase with the teams I've led. But it is also appropriate for the teams I've been a member of.

Belonging to a great team is one of the most rewarding experiences you will ever have on the job. The group you work with can be a tremendous source of joy and support day in and day out, if you allow it to be. The people in your group can be the ones who save your sanity when you are losing it. The folks who make you laugh uncontrollably about all the ridiculousness that occurs in the corporate world. Your peers are rowing in the same boat you are, and so they're likely to be well attuned to the experience and thus can be your greatest source of encouragement.

Of all the teams I've been a member of, the last two in particular have had all the benefits I mention above, and more. And no matter how stressed or overwhelmed or just plain crazy things got at work, it was always worth showing up because of the team I was on.

This part of the book captures the elements of what made each of those team experiences extraordinary. As the wisdom literature says, there really isn't anything new under the sun. The principles and tips discussed are hardly revolutionary. But they *can* revolutionize your work life if you choose to follow them and demonstrate the courage, vulnerability, and truth telling they require, so that you too can have an awesome experience with your peers.

Here they are again for your quick reference:

1. *Fall in like* by inviting colleagues to your home for a meal.

2. Insist on collaboration across functional and business boundaries, and demonstrate it yourself.

3. Tell the truth. Have the courage to go to your peer to resolve a conflict as soon as it arises. Don't let things fester.

4. When you mess up, 'fess up.

5. Ask and offer help, often and proactively.

6. Look for opportunities to praise your peers to the boss and others.

Being a great colleague requires you to care enough to be conscious about your behavior. It requires positive intent on your part and the willingness to "go first." If you have lousy, conflict-filled relationships at work, the first place to look is in the mirror. Sure, it may be that you are surrounded by daft morons, but it just may be that your colleagues see you as a daft moron.

So decide to give some qi, demonstrate a generous spirit, and treat your colleagues the way you want to be treated.

Remember, the only thing you can reliably control or change at your company is yourself.

PART
4

Lead Your Team

ABOUT
"LEAD YOUR TEAM"

SAM WALTON, THE late founder and CEO of Walmart, ushered in a new era of management philosophy using the concept of servant leadership. This concept dates back to about 500 BC, when it appeared in the Chinese spiritual text known as the *Tao Te Ching*. In the 1970s, servant leadership was reintroduced by business writer Robert K. Greenleaf in an influential essay entitled "The Servant as Leader."

For Sam Walton, servant leadership was a very simple, practical concept—and one that he embodied. It was an emphatically down-to-earth approach with all customers, suppliers, and employees (whom he called "associates"). Together with his passion for being on the floor of his stores, this was a radical departure from the executive suite–style management of other large companies.

I spent my first nine years in corporate America at Walmart. Sam Walton's legacy was very much alive and well during my time there, even though he had passed away a few years before my arrival. Sam's management theories had a huge impact on my career and general orientation toward leading others. The concept that I as a leader existed *to remove obstacles* for my people has influenced every team I have ever led.

True, that isn't the only role of a leader. But it's an essential one to keep in mind. Especially if you, like me, have been one of the youngest leaders at your company, or the only female leader, or promoted ahead of your peers, or leading a disparate group of people spanning all age ranges, from millennials to traditionalists, living all over the world. When all else fails, go back to the tenet of servant leadership.

Over the course of my career, I've come across very helpful tools, concepts, and techniques regarding leading a team, the best of which I share with you here. Each is rooted in that singular truth about business mentioned in the previous three parts of this book—that the only thing you can reliably control or change at your company is yourself. This is especially important to remember when leading teams. You can coach, mentor, role model, and create "oxygen in the room" for others to flourish, but fundamentally you can't force someone to change or perform better. That's an inside-out job for everyone.

You can, however, dramatically increase your odds of having a high-performing, mutually caring, respectful, talented, and results-oriented team by following the recommendations in this section. Which will require courageous leadership and truth telling on your part.

The writer Eric Bloom stated, "People join companies and leave managers." (HR leaders around the world continue to remind business colleagues of this every day.) Bloom is right. That's why this section is designed to help you do better and be better. As with the other three parts of the book, applying the materials covered in here will work only if you have the desire to change, grow, and evolve your leadership, and the desire to have a positive impact on those you serve.

This exploration of the topic of leading one's team is clearly not exhaustive—just look at the length of it. Hundreds of books have been written on business leadership over the years. I'm not trying to reinvent the wheel or put a new spin on old stuff. What you will find here is a distilled version of some of the best ideas I have encountered and implemented (but not invented—what a bummer!). Ideas that work incredibly well.

No theory. No academic mumbo jumbo. This stuff actually works. Whether you have reached the rarified air of the C-suite or you are a new manager leading your first team, you'll find that the principles espoused here are universal and applicable.

The tendency I have observed is that, over time and with experience, it is easy to get overly relaxed about building high-performing teams. There's a sense of "I know what I'm doing; I've been at this a long time" or "I'm very senior and thus must be a great leader," resulting in a dismissive attitude about intentionally spending time with direct reports both individually and collectively in order to create the best team possible.

Don't make that mistake. This section is for anyone who leads another human being. No matter the size of the company, or the age or seniority of those involved. Here is what you will find:

Chapter 27 covers what to do in the first two weeks of taking over a new team.

Chapter 28 reframes how to use your monthly one-on-one meetings with your direct reports for shockingly good results.

Chapters 29 and 30 cover both hiring and firing and tried-and-true approaches to doing both significantly better.

Chapter 31 introduces you to the best method for creating and sustaining that most sought-after destination: the high-performing team.

Chapter 32 enumerates how you can lead large-scale change more effectively from day one.

Chapter 33 tackles five common meeting challenges and offers simple solutions to each.

Chapter 34 pulls it all together into a concise recap.

27

A Fresh Start

THERE ARE MANY critical moments associated with being the leader of a team. One of those moments comes at the very beginning of your tenure.

It's a time for you to set a new tone, to demystify who you are, and to get people excited about the new sheriff in town.

The importance of this occasion may seem obvious. But too many leaders allow it to pass them by. One senior executive I know recently joined a new firm and completely overlooked getting in sync with his direct reports during the first two weeks on the job. He was too busy learning about the company, the industry, and his own new boss.

When I asked him how he was approaching his new team, he said off-handedly, "Oh, I'll get to it by the end of the quarter."

I thought, "Mate, those horses will be out of the barn by then. Good luck with yer wrangling!" And, of course, those early months flew by and his biggest on-the-job frustration now is fixing the broken dynamics of his direct report team.

Let's get down to it. Your direct reports want to please you, do good work, and take home a paycheck to their family. They may not like you. They may wish they had got the job you got. They may even think you shouldn't be in a leadership role. But you are, and that's what matters.

Regardless of what your direct reports might think, for as long as they work for you, they still want to please you ... because their jobs depend on it. And while your job is to please *your* boss and support him or her and start contributing meaningfully, the only way you can accomplish that is *through your team.*

> **Productivity naturally slows and anxiety increases any time there is a leadership transition.**

The team's priorities need to be set early in your tenure. Otherwise you've just lost vital time and momentum. Why? Because productivity naturally slows and anxiety increases any time there is a leadership transition.

Chapter 2 in Part 1, "You First," explores the concept of the Personal Declaration. If you've read that chapter and done the introspection work, you are halfway home. Your Personal Declaration—with a few additions—should serve as the foundation of your first two weeks as the leader of your team. During those weeks, you need to accomplish two essential tasks:

1. Have one-on-one discussions with each direct report and share your Personal Declaration with them: who you are, what you value, what's important to you. And invite them to reciprocate.

2. Have a full-team session solely devoted to assimilating you as a leader. This is called a New Leader Assimilation session. It typically takes a few hours and is facilitated by someone other than yourself—a member of the HR team or an external consultant.

YOUR PERSONAL DECLARATION WITH A DIRECT
REPORT—A PRIVATE CONVERSATION

YOUR TIME SPENT one on one with each team member, before pulling your team together as a group, is essential to your success as team leader. You will be able to allay fears about who you are by immediately being open and honest about subjects such as:

- The family you come from, where you were born and raised, details about your siblings.

- The family you're part of now.

- Your passions outside of work.

- Your motto or life philosophy (in one sentence).

- Your values.

- Your greatest strengths—what you're naturally good at.

- Your weaknesses—what you're plain lousy at.

- Your hot buttons and pet peeves.

- What motivates you to come to work every day.

Your direct report may be astonished to have the leader go so deep so fast. Some will be impressed or suspicious—or both. That's okay. The only way your Personal Declaration doesn't serve to build a foundation for your leadership is if you don't tell the truth or if you pontificate or posture (see the tips in Chapter 2 for more on this). As long as what you *do* lines up with what you *say*, team members will be grateful to have these insights.

For those of you who are intensely private, this may feel incredibly uncomfortable and far too revealing. You may think, "I don't want to share all of this personal stuff. I don't want anyone at work to know too much about me. We should just keep the focus on the job." This is an understandable reaction, but I am going to have to respectfully disagree with you.

As a team leader, you have an obligation to create an environment of trust. Without trust, you won't get the best work from your people. And part of building trust is showing vulnerability and being human. This can be taken too far, of course. I'll never forget the first time I tried doing my Personal Declaration to my team as a group, versus the recommended one-on-one (I was going for speed and efficiency—ugh). I got on a roll about my family of origin (not a happy story) and ended up shocking myself and my new team by my over-sharing. Very embarrassing and an important lesson learned. Keep the Personal Declaration personal by doing it individually, and keep your one-pager firmly in front of your face.

> As a team leader, you have an obligation to create an environment of trust. Without trust, you won't get the best work from your people. And part of building trust is showing vulnerability and being human.

A balance between openness and authenticity on the one hand, and appropriate disclosure on the other is essential. You introverts are likely to have no difficulty with this. Extroverts, watch out!

Once you've shared your Personal Declaration, be sure to invite your direct report to share the same level of information with you. A great way to manage this is to share a copy of your declaration with your direct report after talking it through with them. This gives them a reference point for the future but also a framework for them to use in order to share similar information with you. Some will take you up on that right away during the same conversation. Others will want to go away and think about it and then schedule a meeting at which to share more about themselves in a prepared manner.

After these conversations, it's time to get the team together.

NEW LEADER ASSIMILATION—A CRITICAL TEAM CONVERSATION

TOM STREHLE, A gifted HR leader I've had the privilege of working with at both Campbell Soup Company and Jim Beam, designed the New Leader Assimilation process you'll read about here. (I've made slight modifications based on my experience.)

A third party needs to facilitate the New Leader Assimilation session because, for a portion of the time, you will be out of

KEEP IT SIMPLE

Keep the process of sharing your Personal Declaration simple and straightforward. When you first take on the responsibility of leading your team, schedule individual 1:1s. Most leaders do this as an exercise to get to know who is working for them. But now, it is *how* you will use this time that will be different. You don't need to prepare your direct report for the conversation or tell them that you will be doing a Personal Declaration. Have the conversation—you will be role modeling. At the end of sharing, give them your one-pager and invite them to reciprocate.

the room and your team will be asking and answering questions. The facilitator is also a nice neutralizer—they can prompt more in-depth discussions and ensure that courage and openness remain high throughout the experience.

As an HR executive, I've facilitated many of these sessions. I've also experienced the session as a new leader. I love how these sessions accelerate getting a team on the right track from the start.

The table opposite walks you through the process. Following that you'll find a list of suggested questions to use for your session. The total time of the session is approximately three to four hours.

HIRING AN EXTERNAL CONSULTANT

Engaging a third party to facilitate your New Leader Assimilation session is important because your role as the leader is to participate fully and not be worried about asking questions, keeping the process flowing, or any of the other details that a facilitator is tasked with ensuring. Most importantly, there will be times that you will not be in the room with your team and you will need a facilitator to manage your team through the process to make sure you and your team get the most out of the experience.

THE NEW LEADER ASSIMILATION SESSION

PRE-SESSION
Meet with facilitator to review and validate the questions that will be asked, determine the flow of the session, and establish your comfort with the facilitator voicing issues that the team may shy away from.

TEAM SESSION	
ACTION	**TIME (APPROX.)**
1. Leader introduction. You, the leader, introduce the goal of the session (to jumpstart your relationship with your team): explain why they are there and what you want to accomplish. Introduce facilitator and explain their role. Answer any questions. Leave the room.	10 minutes
2. Team activity. Facilitator explains that there are a series of questions—one per large Post-it flip chart along the walls. Each team member is to answer the questions on a Post-it Note and attach to the corresponding flip chart.	1 hour
3. Facilitator debrief with team. Facilitator has a group discussion with the team and reviews each question to ensure members understand the concepts, feedback, and ideas from the team, and to clarify any further thoughts.	30 minutes
4. Facilitator review with leader. Team takes a break. During the break, facilitator meets with you to review team's comments and questions.	30 minutes
5. Group dialogue with leader. Entire group comes back together. You answer the questions, respond to the feedback, and provide next steps if there are any actions to be taken. Facilitator ensures that you are addressing all important issues or concerns that were raised. Team has opportunity to provide follow-up commentary and questions. *This is a conversation, not a monologue, so keep it interactive.*	1 hour
6. Leader expectations. Once you have answered all the questions, if it hasn't already come up, share what dynamics and values you expect the team to display, and any other expectations you have of the entire group, plus how you want team members individually to interact and behave. Make sure to clarify what is acceptable and what is not.	15 minutes
7. Wrap-up. Thank team members for their openness and honesty. Express your enthusiasm for being a part of this team. Thank facilitator.	5 minutes

Now go have a cocktail and dinner with your team—you've all earned it!

Session Questions

Here's a list of questions to pose in the session. Feel free to include additional questions or modify the ones here. This is art, not science. The key is to actually have the session.

- What do you want to know about [leader's name]?
- What do you need from [leader's name]?
- What are your expectations of [leader's name]?
- What does [leader's name] know about your team?
- What do you want [leader's name] to know about your team?
- What worries you as a team member?
- What are the key challenges and underlying issues facing the team?
- What are the key success factors in the team reaching its goals?
- How effective is the team in supporting its customers?
- What is working well, and not working well, with the team?
- What would you like to see more of and less of?
- What changes do you believe [leader's name] is going to make?
- What is the preferred amount of discretion and autonomy versus control between [leader's name] and the team?
- How do we move quickly from "forming" to "norming" as a team?*

Leader Expectations

One part of the conversation that deserves extra emphasis is that about leader expectations (Step 6 in the table on the

---

* In 1965 Bruce Tuckman devised the "forming, storming, norming, performing" model of group development. His premise was that all teams go through these phases, although the pace at which they move through the phases varies. Many later team models were based on Tuckman's original work.

previous page). This step can easily get glossed over if you are not careful. You need to come prepared with your point of view on what the guardrails for behavior will be for this team—the behaviors you expect to see and the behaviors you will not tolerate. Many leaders fail here because they assume good behavior is a given. It's not. People need to be reminded of expectations. As the saying goes, "Repetition is the best form of emphasis."

You may choose to anchor your comments in the company's values.

> Many leaders fail because they assume good behavior is a given. It's not. People need to be reminded of expectations.

Do this only if these values are clearly articulated and understood by those working for you. Bottom line? Be clear. Remember, you are trying to accelerate effectiveness and productivity, reduce ambiguity and anxiety, and quickly establish the way things are going to operate going forward.

Encourage questions from your new team and make sure to explain why you are taking the stance you are. Your intent is to minimize future surprises.

Tips for Making the New Leader Assimilation Session Work
Here are four tips for a successful New Leader Assimilation session:

- *Stay relaxed and open.* Try not to get defensive or be offended by what comes up. This is a leadership *moment* and you want to demonstrate your humanity—that you are relatively normal and have the team's best interest at heart. Don't go all weird and formal on the group. If you are uncomfortable or awkward, the team will know it and clam up.

- *Keep a sense of humor.* You aren't perfect, and no one expects you to be. Enjoy the dialogue and be grateful for the courage your team displays and the trust its members demonstrate by simply showing up in good faith and participating. Remember, you are at the beginning of a journey with this group of people. During one of my New Leader Assimilation processes, a group of senior leaders I had recently inherited to lead wanted to know first and foremost when the "What do you want to know about Mindy?" question was posed, why I drove a pickup truck. Of all the questions I had anticipated they might ask, that was not one of them! Totally cracked me up. It's still one of my favorite memories.

- *Keep it simple.* Make sure the facilitator you bring in does not over-engineer the session. If the facilitator starts to complicate matters as you are doing your preparatory meetings with them, graciously cancel their services and find someone else. You need a level-headed, credible person who can shepherd your crew through the entire exercise and debrief you on what transpired when you were out of the room, so the right partner is critical. Then you can provide the insight and information your team needs.

- *Be plainspoken and down-to-earth.* Do not pontificate. Or posture. Or lecture. Or condescend. People are smart. People can smell BS a mile away. Your team will appreciate how this process may be uncomfortable for you. The more authentic, respectful, and kind you are, the more appreciative and responsive the team will be.

YOU ARE THE ultimate beneficiary of investing this time with your team, both individually and collectively, because you will know very early in your tenure what's on the minds of your team members.

The obvious benefit for the team is a chance to see how you are going to lead, and to connect with your humanity and humility. It takes courage to have frank discussions so early on. But it eliminates so much wasted time and energy that any discomfort your direct reports or you may feel is well worth it. Imagine how good it will feel to have a real handle on your team by week three on the job.

KEEP IT GOING

A great way to sustain the level of insight and transparency achieved in the New Leader Assimilation session is to have a direct report who participated in the session take new team members (who joined the team afterward) through what was asked and discussed. You will, of course, have done your Personal Declaration with each new team member in the first week they work for you. That, coupled with a peer sharing the process of the team conversation, and the dialogue, will be an excellent addition to their orientation.

28

Getting Connected—and Staying Connected— with Your Direct Reports

ONE OF THE CEOS I advise said to me in our very first conversation, "Mindy, I have no idea what my people *really* think of me. Sometimes as I watch them leave my office after a conversation we've had, I sit and wonder what's really going on in their heads." This CEO went on to lament that he had to intervene at critical junctures in client work, on projects of strategic importance, and generally struggled to even take a vacation because his senior people "didn't operate at a senior enough level."

Being in tune and staying connected with the people you lead is essential to getting solid business results. That's a given: you get results through people.

"Do they know you feel this way?" I asked.

"No way! I wouldn't want to disengage them—they work too hard!"

"How do you expect anything to change or improve if you aren't willing to tell them the truth?"

(Sheepish laugh.) "Uh...that's why I hired you."

Being in tune and staying connected with the people you lead is essential to getting solid business results. That's a given: you get results through people. And leading leaders requires something even more.

The more senior you get, the more that success becomes far less about technical excellence and far more about your ability to influence, lead, collaborate across functional boundaries, and take an enterprise-wide view of the business—versus caring only about the patch you are responsible for.

Let me repeat myself: The more senior you become, the less technical skills matter and the more leadership counts. The same is true for the leaders you are leading right now. It is far more likely that the barriers to their advancement—to replacing you!—have less to do with any gaps they may have in their technical skills and a lot more to do with gaps in their relationship and stakeholder management, in their influencing skills, in their ability to collaborate, and in their general leadership capability.

> **Truth telling is the commodity in shortest supply in the corporate world today.**

But for executives and senior leaders of all stripes, having direct conversations about these gaps is daunting and tends to be avoided. I fundamentally believe that truth telling is the commodity in shortest supply in the corporate world today. Why? Because addressing leadership or interpersonal gaps can be awkward. These topics seem more subjective—they can't be precisely quantified. Your people are working hard, making sacrifices, getting good results. And generally, you just wish your people would "get it," so you can get on with running the business. It is far easier to address technical and functional skill gaps than it is to address the "softer" elements of effective business conduct, namely human interaction skills or EQ (emotional intelligence).

The risk to this approach is obvious. The very areas that get in the way of advancement to the senior-most roles are the very topics that senior executives tend to avoid. Which results in disappointed people, outside hiring, and a poor-performance culture.

If you are a mid-level manager leading a team of individual contributors, your challenge is the same. Because no matter your level in the organization or of those you lead, you need to have effective coaching and development conversations with your people. You know you do. The challenge is doing it *well*. Now I'm going to let you in on a secret method: an easier way for you to have higher-quality conversations with the people you lead about the things that really matter.

And you are going to apply this method in the most mundane of environments—the classic monthly 1:1 meeting. Most if not all leaders in the modern corporate world have monthly 1:1s with their direct reports. These meetings either can be a tremendous source of information, a way to get and stay connected on a meaningful level and to provide coaching and development in a naturally occurring way *or* they can be routine transactional conversations about work—essentially, the same conversations you have daily and weekly, only now under the banner of the monthly 1:1. So how do you transform these meetings so they are the former rather than the latter?

THE SCALE OF 1-10 QUESTION

THE SCALE OF 1–10 Question will dramatically change the quality of the monthly 1:1 meeting. It will both serve as truth serum for your direct report so that you learn what they think of you and your leadership, and it will provide you with an opportunity to painlessly highlight your direct report's development areas and gaps. It's an easy, stress-free way to have courageous, truth-telling conversations about those dreaded leadership and EQ topics.

The question is designed to be used in *two ways* during the monthly 1:1—that is, there are two parts to the process. But in order for it to work, you have to *go first*. This means checking *in* with your direct report so that you earn the right to check *on* them by demonstrating that you have the courage to expose yourself to scrutiny first. Let's take a look at how part 1 works.

Part 1: Checking *In*
Ready to have squirm-free dialogue about your leadership effectiveness, so that you never again need to wonder what your people really think of you because you'll know? There are five steps to part 1, once pleasantries have been exchanged:

Step 1
You, the leader: "On a scale of 1 to 10, with 1 being lousy and 10 being fabulous, how would you rate our relationship now?"

Step 2
Your direct report: He or she provides a number, with rationale. If your direct report fails to provide you a reason for the number they are giving, ask them explicitly.

Step 3
You, the leader (whatever the response may be): "Okay, what can I do differently to move our relationship to a 10?" Then stop talking and listen.

Step 4

Your direct report: He or she answers.
When your direct report is finished speaking, respond with your
point of view.

Step 5

You, the leader:
If you agree: *"Thank you for sharing how you feel and how I*
can improve. I am happy to make that adjustment."
If you disagree: *"Thank you for telling me how you feel and*
what you'd like me to do differently. I really appreciate it. In
this instance, however, I can't agree with you because [reason
you can't agree]."

The first few times you ask the Scale of 1–10 Question, you
may get dubious looks from your direct reports. But you can
earn their trust by genuinely caring about their answers—and
by responding honestly. In so doing, you'll learn the truth about
what is and what isn't working in terms of what you are doing.

One of my direct reports, a seasoned veteran significantly
older than me and big on hierarchy, said to me, "Oh, I'd say we
are a 9 or 10. Everything's good, boss."

I didn't for a second believe this because we were disagreeing
vehemently on a particular issue and I knew he was upset. So I
said, "Actually, Joe, I anticipated you would rate our relationship
about a 3 right now because you were clearly upset with me the
other day when we disagreed on that issue. How are you feeling
about that now?"

He then admitted that he was in fact ticked off at me, and
we were able to get at what was bugging him and, more importantly, how we were going to operate going forward. At the end of
the discussion he said, "You know, Mindy, I thought this 1-to-10

question was kind of stupid when you first started asking me, but now I look forward to it because it gives me a way to calibrate where we're at. Next time I will rate you a 1 or 2 when I'm mad at you like I was today and know that it'll be okay to."

See how amazing this is? It's truth serum! A simple number allows you to bring up thorny topics, resolve unspoken issues, and keep the conversation productive. If you are a decent leader and treat your people with respect, you will always know exactly what your direct reports are thinking about your leadership.

Remember, though, that you have to (1) care what they actually think and (2) tell the truth. If you think they are blowing smoke or off base, you have to tell them. It is truth-telling time.

IT'S NORMAL TO FEEL RESISTANT

I know what you're thinking right now: "Mindy, this is really weird and awkward. My direct report is going to think I am in airy-fairy land and they're not going to really tell me the truth. Besides, I'm a big, bad leader. My business is good. I know my people. Why would *I* need to do this?"

You're right—the first few times you pose the Scale of 1–10 Question, it will likely feel a little awkward or slightly unnerving, or you may even feel a bit ridiculous asking it. That's normal and to be expected. *What it's not is an excuse to not ask it.*

To work through that, simply preface what you are about to do by telling your direct report:

> *"I'm going to try out a new technique I recently learned in a terrific leadership book I read. It is designed to help improve my leadership effectiveness and it's a way to check in on our relationship. I'm going to be asking you this question every month, and I really want to know what you think."*

And then ask the question.

For those of you leading some really tough nuts, it may take a few times for them to feel comfortable with answering the question honestly, but ultimately most people will be thrilled you care enough about the relationship to even ask it, and they will be even more impressed with your courage to truly listen and respond.

Now you may be thinking, "Mindy, this is nice, but I've worked at my company for a very long time. I've got people who have worked for me for 10, 15, 20 years. We know each other. We can finish each other's sentences. We don't need some prescribed question in order to have conversations."

Long-term working relationships have many benefits—and drawbacks. The biggest drawback is that the chummier you are, the harder it is to have tough conversations and give genuine feedback so that your people get better or for you to receive feedback on your leadership effectiveness. Our human inclination is to avoid difficult conversations, especially with folks we really like or know well. We think it's just not worth the pain. But there is a huge cost to that avoidance, as the next story illustrates.

Time Out: The Junkyard Dog

Before we get to Part 2 of the Scale of 1–10 Question process, let me tell you a story. It's one of the more disappointing stories I have heard and is about a debate that ensued among an executive team regarding internal candidates after their chief supply-chain executive left the company. One senior supply-chain leader—let's call him Eric—who worked for a region president was a serious contender. He was brilliant—operationally savvy and a super-creative problem solver. One of the best. Except for one thing.

Eric was what I call a "junkyard dog." He pissed people off. A lot. He was a terrible collaborator, coming across as condescending. He had a nasty "bite." Nobody had trained him or expected him to behave any differently, so he didn't. And his behavior was never dealt with by his superiors because he was so smart.

During the succession discussion, every member of the executive team acknowledged that Eric was intelligent and talented. Indeed, he received generous retention awards to stay at the business. Yet not one of the C-suite executives, including Eric's own boss, could imagine him on their top team—because of his abrasive approach and style. It would signal the wrong thing to the organization.

Question for you: Were Eric's development areas new news to the executive team? Nope. Not new.

Did his direct manager, the region president, know that Eric had these gaps? Yes, he did.

Did that leader have tough conversations with Eric to tell him to knock off being a jerk and get his attitude toward colleagues in check? No, he did not.

Why not?

The region president made excuses for Eric and would smooth things over when Eric caused trouble through his lack of collaboration or condescension. His leader excused Eric's behavior because he had known Eric for years, including at a different organization. He would lightly or carefully talk to his junkyard dog but avoided really getting into it because he didn't want to disengage Eric, since Eric was getting excellent results in certain areas.

The executive team had also discussed Eric's development areas repeatedly each year and were generally satisfied with the glimmers of improvement because, while they talked a good succession game, they didn't anticipate a *real* need. They kept labeling him "ready now" on succession plans, but when the moment actually arrived, every single executive backed off from that rating and said they couldn't take the risk. They would need to hire from the outside. Because you couldn't in good conscience put a junkyard dog onto the executive team.

Unfortunately, this is not an uncommon story. I bet you know some junkyard dogs at your company.

The tragedy is that, had the region president had the courage along the way to have the brave discussions—to tell the truth to Eric, give him tough feedback and coaching, and expect his behavior to improve, he could have promoted him. And guess what? All Eric wants is to get on the C-suite team. He has worked his whole career for it. He is smart enough and experienced enough for it. But because no one has told him the truth—that it takes more than technical excellence to get in the top job, and that it matters how you treat people and work with them—he has missed his opportunity.

What do you think Eric is going to do? Stay or go?

That's right. Go.

Because he is smart, ambitious, and now, also angry. He thought he was a highflier. He was told he was one! He was brought in on the promise of advancement. He was showered with money to stay and told he was mission critical to the company. But when the company had the chance to promote him to a top job, it took a pass.

Part 2: Checking *On*

Eric would not have been passed over for promotion if his leader knew the secret to having stress-free development conversations with him. There is a simple way to ensure your department (or organization) has genuinely "ready now" talent.

Part 2 of the Scale of 1–10 Question method is an opportunity to shine a light on your direct report's development areas. It is the most pain-free way to have those tough conversations that you tend to avoid, and you are going to do it in that same monthly 1:1 session.

You see, once you have demonstrated your courage and vulnerability by *going first* and doing a relationship check-*in* with your direct report, you have earned the right to ask the same of them, to check *on* them. You can use the Scale of 1–10 Question to dig in.

There are many potential development gaps. Some you personally may observe in your direct report, some you may have heard others complain about (even if you yourself don't see them). To keep things simple, I've listed only four of the most common development areas. You'll also find on the next page follow-up questions, to be used in conjunction with the Scale of 1–10 Question to spark quality, courageous dialogue in a non-stressful way. You can modify these questions to fit the areas in which your people need to improve.

COMMON DEVELOPMENT AREAS

- Self-Awareness/Team Leadership. How aware is the leader about how good a leader they are, and how in tune is the leader with how their team feels about them?

- Peer Collaboration. How clearly does the leader "read" their impact on peers and colleagues?

- Customer Engagement. How effective is the leader in calibrating the relationship health of internal or external relationships?

- Team/Organization Culture. How intentioned is the leader in creating a healthy, high-performing organization culture?

PART 2 FOLLOW-UP QUESTIONS

SELF-AWARENESS/TEAM LEADERSHIP	PEER COLLABORATION
1. How would you rate your current effectiveness in leading your team on a scale of 1 to 10, with 1 being lousy and 10 being fabulous? 2. How would your team rate you? 3. Why those numbers? 4. What do you think you need to do more or less of to move closer to a 10? 5. Where are you stuck personally? What are you struggling with in terms of your team?	1. You are currently doing a lot of work with X function/department. How would you rate the quality of your collaboration on a scale of 1 to 10, with 1 being lousy and 10 being fabulous? 2. Why that number? 3. What do you need to do differently to give yourself a 10? 4. What have you successfully tried in other cross-functional relationships that could be applied here? 5. What are you struggling with?
CUSTOMER ENGAGEMENT	**TEAM/ORGANIZATION CULTURE**
1. How would you rate your relationship with X customer on a scale of 1 to 10, with 1 being lousy and 10 being fabulous? 2. How would your customer rate you? 3. Why those numbers? 4. What do you think you need to do differently to move your relationship closer to a 10? 5. What is getting in the way?	1. How would you rate the culture of the team (or department or organization) you lead on a scale of 1 to 10, with 1 being lousy and 10 being fabulous? 2. What data support that number? 3. What needs to change for the culture to be a 10? 4. What have you tried? 5. What is getting in the way of making changes?

EXAMPLE DIALOGUE

Let's take a look at a sample conversation between me as the leader and Fictional Faith, my direct report, so you can get a sense of how the method works. This example involves the category of Self-Awareness/Team Leadership:

Me: *How would you rate your current effectiveness in leading your team on a scale of 1 to 10, Faith, with 10 being fabulous and 1 being lousy?*

Faith: *I'd give myself a 7 or 8.*

Me: *Why do you give yourself that number?*

Faith: *Because everyone seems to be getting along well, and there hasn't been a lot of drama lately.*

Me: *When I go to your team and ask them to rate you as a leader on a scale of 1 to 10, how will they rate you?*

Faith: *A couple people would probably give me a slightly lower number. Everyone else likely a 7 or 8.*

Me: *What do you need to do more or less of to move closer to a 10?*

Faith: *Well, I guess I could intercede earlier when Roberta and Sam can't agree on how to divvy up budget dollars. That is when we have the biggest team explosions. And it would be Roberta and Sam that would give me lower ratings, I think.*

Me: *Where are you stuck?*

Faith: *Well, I hate knowing that whatever decision I make is going to upset one of them. We've been through this over and*

over again, and I just wish they would figure it out themselves
versus me having to be the referee. It stresses me out.

Me: *I've noticed you do seem stressed out and kind of freeze*
whenever there is team tension or drama. But I also see you
doing this in other areas.

Notice that throughout this example, you as the leader are
primarily *listening and prompting*, rather than talking. Your direct
report is doing all the work. The magic of this approach is that
the pressure is taken off you.

Ask open-ended questions that elicit introspection and self-awareness.

There will come a natural moment—
an opportunity for truth telling—when
you may say something like, "Interesting perspective, Faith. If I were to rate
you at this moment, I would give you a 5 because you are having
more of a negative impact on your team than you may realize."
And you are off.

As you can see, you could take any area where your direct
report needs to grow, and which you need to have a conversation with them about, and use the Scale of 1–10 Question, along
with good follow-up questions, to have a substantive discussion
about the real issues.

This is more art than science. The key is to ask open-ended
questions that elicit introspection and self-awareness. Many
times, just asking these questions will result in your direct
report verbalizing issues and solutions without you having to
raise them or tell them what to do.

And if there are problems you need to resolve or have feedback to give, this is a natural way to enter into that conversation.

MAKING THE MOST OF THE MONTHLY 1:1

I HAD ONE underperforming direct report who gave me a really low number on the 1 to 10 scale because of feedback I had recently given her. When I asked how to move our relationship from 2 to 10, she said I should recant my feedback because I was wrong.

It was a golden opportunity to bluntly say that I wasn't going to change my mind, that her performance was unacceptable, that I expected her to change her behavior—and that I believed she could if she chose to. But, further, if she was unwilling to change, that was a separate issue and we probably needed to have a different conversation.

> Distinguishing your monthly 1:1s as a way to improve your leadership impact and also to grow and develop those you lead will result in a huge return on the time invested.

While this was not an enjoyable exchange, it did prompt this person to leave the organization. When she resigned, she said to me, "Mindy, I don't much like you, and I disagree about your assessment of my performance. But I have to say, you are the most direct, clear, and consistent boss I have ever had."

I took that as a massive compliment. I was glad to see her move on to a position that would better fit her skills and abilities.

We all know leadership isn't about being liked or making friends, yet it's easy to forget that and secretly yearn for approval from our team. Asking the Scale of 1–10 Question, along with the follow-up questions, is a fantastic way to calibrate your leadership impact and create a space for powerful conversations.

In today's highly connected environment, contact with your direct reports is often "just-in-time," with the daily or weekly interaction focused on whatever needs to get done. The pace is fast. Interactions with your direct reports can become transactional and only issue-of-the-day-oriented.

Distinguishing your monthly 1:1s as a way to improve your leadership impact and also to grow and develop those you lead will result in a huge return on the time invested—in a natural, stress-free manner.

In my experience, the single greatest use of these sessions is to have:

1. A relationship check-in with you and your direct report.

2. A discussion of the state of the team your direct report is leading.

3. Your direct report's assessment of their own interactions with peers, colleagues, customers, and other key stakeholders.

A monthly meeting should help your direct report grow as a leader. It should allow you to stay connected to the culture your direct reports are creating within their departments. And it should help you tweak your relationships with your direct reports so they stay engaged to the greatest possible degree. This approach will signal that you care about *how* they do their jobs as much as *what* they get done. And that you care how you are behaving and impacting them as their leader.

People join companies and leave managers (as writer Eric Bloom observed). My experience is that when leaders demonstrate their caring for their people (like this approach accomplishes when effectively applied), their people experience significantly higher job satisfaction and longevity in the role, and the poor performers on the team tend to self-select out at a much quicker rate. So, yes, schedule and keep your monthly 1:1s with your direct reports. But don't fill those meeting with everyday updates and tactical business items. Instead, use the time for quality discussions about how you can better lead them and how they can improve their own leadership impact.

29

Casting—Getting the Right People in the Right Roles

STARED AT HIM. Stared at him hard. I thought to myself, "I think he'll be okay. He's got the experience. I *do* see some question marks... but this position has been open so long. How bad can it be?"

It can be pretty bad, folks. I made the classic hiring mistake I had, throughout my career, preached against doing. I knew in my gut that I was "hiring desperate," but I really was desperate. So I paid for it big time, as did the rest of my team—with a painful year of trying to make it work with this vice president who should never have been hired to begin with.

All because I closed my eyes to what I knew to be true and went ahead anyway.

It wasn't long after this hiring debacle that I came across The Best Book Ever on hiring. It's called *Who: The A Method for Hiring*, by Geoff Smart and Randy Street. It features simple, straight-forward, behavior-based interviewing techniques, along with "truth serum" screening questions and dummy-proof interviewing guidelines. Awesome! I read it in one weekend. On Monday, I told my team we were going to utilize Smart and Street's hiring method. If it worked as well as I expected, we would roll it out to the entire company.

I'll never forget the first interview at which I used the book. I actually had it there with me, with all my highlighting and Post-it Notes, to make sure I didn't screw things up. It worked like a charm.

One of the C-suite executives who we hired subsequent to my *Who* conversion referred to his two-and-a-half-hour interview with me as the "Mindy meat grinder." Just surviving it was an achievement, he said. But he also knew he wanted to join our company because our company clearly took *hiring right* very seriously.

WHY IT'S WORTH YOUR TIME TO TAKE YOUR TIME

YOUR NUMBER ONE job as a leader is *getting the right people in the right roles*. When you mess this up, you cause yourself and everyone around you heaps of pain. Don't you get ticked off when your boss hires the wrong person and you have to deal with a less-than-stellar peer?

> Casting correctly requires time, discipline, and patience. There are no shortcuts.

What's more, hiring mistakes cost companies massive amounts of money. In a *Fast Company* article, Tony Hsieh, legendary entrepreneur and CEO of online retailer Zappos.com, states that his past bad hires have cost his company "well over $100 million." The same article refers to a survey of 6,000 hiring professionals worldwide, in which more than half said their companies have felt the effects of hiring errors. Twenty-seven percent of the US employers surveyed said that even one bad hire costs their company more than $50,000.*

But forget that for a minute. Because I know you. You're like me. You're busy. You're stressed. You are time-starved. And the arguments around dollars and costs to the company don't really resonate when you are drowning in work and you have open roles in your department.

I get it. I really do. But it's not an excuse. Casting correctly requires time, discipline, and patience. There are no shortcuts.

> **As the leader of a team, when it comes to casting your team, it is your accountability—and your failure—if it doesn't work out.**

In moviemaking, casting the right person for the right role is taken very seriously. Entire movie franchises rely on getting it right. There are A-list actors who would be abysmal if placed in a role that didn't maximize their strengths. And how many times have you read a terrific book and had a vision of the main characters and then, when the movie came out, you were bitterly disappointed because the actors weren't a good fit?

Casting in business is the same. There are many smart, talented professionals. No matter how much you may hear about the talent shortage, that's truly not the issue. The key is having the right process and taking the appropriate amount of time to do the following three steps before casting for the role.

THE THREE-STEP PROCESS TO CASTING CORRECTLY

Step 1: Define the role's outcomes and deliverables—in other words, the work produced by this role and that work's strategic importance to the department or company.

---

* Rachel Gillett, "Infographic: How Much a Bad Hire Will Actually Cost You," *Fast Company*, April 8, 2014.

Step 2: Candidly capture the culture and environment in which the role operates (this is not the time to sugarcoat what it's like for the person in the role to be successful), along with the culture the company aspires to.

Step 3: Interview candidates against the criteria outlined in steps 1 and 2, and look for evidence of when and where they have demonstrated the work product and characteristics you've defined as important.

It is both this simple and this hard to cast right. These three steps take time. They take thought. They take planning.

So many times I hear about leaders writing slipshod job descriptions for a new opening in their department. They pass off the job of defining the role to HR, stay intermittently involved in the selection process, or interview sloppily. And then, when the person ends up failing, they blame HR for a bad hire or are shocked that the person didn't work out.

This is time for some serious truth telling... from me to you. As the leader of a team, when it comes to casting your team, it is your accountability—and your failure—if it doesn't work out. You simply cannot outsource it.

No matter how much you want to blame HR, just like every other area of the business you run, you and those whom you lead have to live with the decisions that you make. You can be supported and augmented by your HR partner, but it's your job, not theirs, to cast correctly.

AVOID THE NUMBER ONE INTERVIEWING MISTAKE

ONE SENIOR LEADER shared with me a story about how her brother interviewed for a position at the very large global company where she happened to be a member of the C-suite executive team. This executive was not part of the interviewing process, nor did the people interviewing her brother know they were related.

At the conclusion of the interviewing process, her brother debriefed her on the eight leaders he had met with (all of whom she knew) and his experience of the company as a result. He said, "Sis, I've heard a lot about your company from you over the years, so I was really excited about the opportunity to potentially join. After going through this process, though, I am less excited. In fact, I don't think I'm interested."

"Why not? What happened?" his sister asked, surprised.

"Only one of the eight people I interviewed with asked me good, tough questions that related to the job I would be doing and then talked candidly about the role and company. The other seven talked about themselves almost the entire time and seemed more concerned with demonstrating how smart they were than getting to know me and listening."

Overtalking versus asking good questions and then listening to the response is epidemic in the corporate world. Forget all the crazy questions you hear about people asking. What is far more prevalent and insidious is the pontificating. You have only a short time to really dig into the candidate's credentials and relevant work experience. Spending this time by not being prepared and by then talking rather than listening (the two are related) not only squanders your opportunity to gather the information you need but also turns off the candidate.

WOULD YOU WORK FOR THIS PERSON?

ONE OF THE best tests I can give myself when casting someone in a role that reports to me—whether an outside hire into the company or an internal candidate—is to ask myself if I would be willing to work for this person.

It is a provocative way to think about talent placement. When my response is an immediate no, it forces me to pause and reflect on why or why not. Oftentimes, this gatekeeping question has saved me from making a desperate hire or helped me clearly identify the development gaps that will need to be shored up in order to make this person successful.

The question forces me to get real with myself and challenge whether I am hiring tough enough. Casting correctly means you are putting people in roles where they not only are able to perform brilliantly in those roles but also have additional capability to do far more for the company in the long term.

BUSINESS RESULTS THROUGH PEOPLE

LEGIONS OF BOOKS have been written on the topic of hiring. After 20 years in the business world, I think that Geoff Smart and Randy Street's *Who: The A Method for Hiring* is the best. Whether you choose to invest time and focus by reading it and applying the authors' well-laid-out process is up to you. You will still get tremendously improved results simply by implementing the three steps highlighted in this chapter.

Either way, you're going to end up eating what you cook. Building a great team, just like cooking a great meal, takes planning, time, and effort. When well done, the result is delicious.

30

"You're Fired"

HAVE YOU EVER delayed firing someone because you hoped they would choose to leave on their own?

Or told yourself, "I know that person has got to go, but we are just too busy right now to get rid of that person. I will deal with it when things ease up."

We've all done it.

Firing someone is one of a leader's toughest tasks.

As discussed in the previous chapter, casting correctly in business, just like casting Hollywood stars in a movie, is all about getting stellar talent into key roles and arguably is your most important leadership job. And in order to create space for the best casting, it is sometimes necessary to let go of someone who at one point was good enough but no longer is.

> **Firing someone is one of a leader's toughest tasks.**

While you know this, you struggle with it. You may even make it more difficult on yourself by holding the mistaken belief that you are *doing something* to that person.

In one conversation with a senior leader about this topic, he explained to me at great length why he couldn't fire a consistently underperforming employee. The employee was going through a divorce, and the leader would have felt guilty about firing him. It would be a terrible thing to do him. It would be *insensitive.*

While I appreciate the sentiment, I completely disagree. If you have clearly communicated expectations and yet the underperformance remains chronic, it's time to take action. Avoiding doing so because of empathy for the employee who is doing a lousy job (as this man was long before his divorce) puts more pressure on many others in your department who are doing their best. It is simply not fair to the rest of your team if you avoid your leadership responsibilities and hope weak links leave on their own.*

Here's the deal: chronic underperformers tend to always have an excuse. And because you want to be liked, you may allow yourself to be manipulated and let poor performance go unaddressed. This negatively impacts many people, all in the name of supposed compassion or sensitivity.

You have probably heard people talk about the Pareto principle in leadership—namely that 20 percent of your people get 80 percent of your results. I've also found it to be true that 20 percent of your people are likely giving you 100 percent of your headaches!

An excellent article published by *Inc.* magazine makes this point. The author, the CEO of a tech startup, writes:

---

* David Cottrell skillfully describes this principle in his short easy-to-read-but-packed-with-practical-wisdom book entitled *Monday Morning Leadership.*

I have never once regretted firing someone. I've never looked back on a close decision that resulted in someone getting fired and thought, "Maybe we should have kept that person." One hundred percent of the time, I look back on a close decision and think, "we should have fired him much earlier." I've often felt very bad about firing someone. Terrible, even. But I've never regretted it.*

Research substantiates this perspective. In an interview with *Harvard Business Review*, the CEO of a major corporation said that a top consistent regret of new CEOs is their not having fired people fast enough:

They almost always say, "I knew in my gut that was not going to work with that individual, and I wish I had trusted that gut feeling and made that decision faster."†

If you have clearly communicated expectations and yet the underperformance remains chronic, it's time to take action. Take a courage pill—and remember that one of your most important responsibilities is to *get the right people into the right roles*. You cannot cast correctly, as discussed in the previous chapter, if you are unwilling to "call it" when you know it is time for someone to go.

THE KEY TO MAKING FIRING EASIER

SO, HOW TO reframe this most difficult of leadership tasks?

---

* Phil Libin, "More Than You Want to Know about Hiring," *Inc.*, December 4, 2012.
† David Astorino, as quoted by Max Nisen, "These Are the People Most Likely to Get Canned if a New CEO Arrives," *Business Insider*, July 8, 2013.

Eliminating the unuseful belief that you are *doing something* to the underperformer you lead is the first step in moving forward. Then keep the following key fact in the forefront of your mind:

The person you are firing has behaved their way to that outcome.

You are not doing anything to them at all. They are experiencing the natural consequences of their own choices. You are not "playing God" simply by being the agent of the result of those consequences. You are not the one consistently delivering poor performance—they are!

Whenever I've had to terminate team members during my career, I've also tried to remember that I am releasing them to their greater good. By leaving a position that didn't work out, they are free to go where they will be a better fit. Happier. More fulfilled.

Most people who are fired for underperformance weren't that happy in the job to begin with and were struggling. You are effectively ending that struggle.

And know this: your refusal to let go people who have behaved their way to that outcome, which effectively blocks your ability to bring in stellar talent, conveys a lot about you as a leader.

IT'S TIME TO THINK ABOUT YOUR TEAM

THERE IS NO better time than the present to spend a few moments reflecting on the team that reports to you. This exercise is simple. Consider the following two questions.

Question 1: If you could wave a magic wand over your team and simply "disappear" your underperformers—being guaranteed no drama or pain—which people would be gone?

Question 2: As you consider your team, do you have stellar talent in the key roles on your team—the talent and capability required for you to succeed over the next one to two years?

Now write down the names of the people you think need to go:

Name: Why they are still here:

_____   _____

_____   _____

_____   _____

Okay. You've identified the people. Now on to the harder part of this exercise. I want you to write down, next to each of the names you've written above, the *reason they are still working for you.*

DID YOU WRITE down something along the lines of "We're too busy," or something to do with the time not being right?

How about "I feel guilty"? Or "I want to give them one more chance"? How about "I haven't really had the tough conversations with them to let them know that if they don't improve they need to go"?

There are myriad reasons for your not having acted on what you know to be true.

You are not alone in your reluctance to take action. But that is no excuse not to. Acknowledge your discomfort and then remember that your employee has *behaved* their way into the outcome they are experiencing.

IT'S YOUR CALL, AND IT'S TIME TO MAKE ONE

NO ONE LIKES to fire people. You will lose sleep over it. It's upsetting and stressful. I've been there many times, and it doesn't get easier. But it is still critical to do, and in order for your team to thrive well into the future and deliver great results, it is imperative that you take action sooner rather than later.

Closing your eyes to under-performance by a team member demonstrates your own underper-formance as a leader. You will be respected by your team for doing what you are being paid to do—which is *lead*. Make the tough calls. Build the best possible team. Cast as well as you can.

> Closing your eyes to under-performance by a team member demonstrates your own underperformance as a leader.

Changing how you think about firing can ease a lot of the mental pain associated with this difficult decision.

31

Great Teams Don't Just Happen

ONE OF THE best compliments I've ever received came from a boss, who said, "Mindy, you've taken B+ players and turned them into an A+ team."

While I didn't entirely agree with him on his B+ rating of some of my people, I greatly appreciated the observation, as this particular team was such a joy to work with and really got the job done.

What was the secret sauce?

I followed Patrick Lencioni's process for creating and maintaining a high-performing team, which he lays out in his insightful book *The Five Dysfunctions of a Team*. At 224 short pages, this leadership fable is a fast, compelling read that provides practical and immediately actionable advice on how to take your team on a journey from dysfunction to high function.

Every team will benefit from going through Lencioni's process, which forces all members to be 1,000 percent engaged in how the team operates—thereby achieving results for the business.

Some teams struggle with intra-team politics. Some teams have a few people who really do all the work. Some teams are generally well intentioned but not aligned with the goals of the company or the priorities you have established. And some teams are severely dysfunctional. No matter where on the spectrum your team operates, and no matter who you think you may need to fire or hire, it is imperative that you invest the time to have the direct and quality conversations that Lencioni's process initiates. Even if you have a team of A players, this process is essential for the team to perform at its absolute best.

> **Delaying spending time with your team to work on increasing the team's collective impact is a grave leadership error.**

It is too easy for people to be passengers in their daily experience at work. When you, as the leader, carve out the time to discuss and agree *how the team will operate*, you send a clear message that being a member of your team is going to require something more than what your direct reports may be used to.

IT'S EASIER THAN YOU THINK

THE VERY NOTION of taking their team through this process—the journey from dysfunction to high function—overwhelms many leaders. After all, they are drowning in the day-to-day workload.

While I empathize, delaying spending time with your team to work on increasing the team's collective impact is a grave leadership error. Devoting a relatively small amount of time to defining, and aligning to, qualities of a high-functioning, healthy, high-performing team will yield huge payoffs in terms of team delivery.

Lencioni frames the journey as overcoming these five dysfunctions:

1. Absence of trust

2. Fear of conflict

3. Lack of commitment

4. Avoidance of accountability

5. Inattention to results

His approach, which is laid out simply in both the book and the accompanying participant workbook,* leads you and your team through a series of practical, thought-provoking activities that prompt all team members to take full ownership of their responsibilities and contribute to creating the environment whereby each team member is focused on meeting and exceeding performance expectations.

I'm sure that as you scan the above list of dysfunctions you can begin to fantasize about what it would be like to *not* have any of these characteristics describe your team. They are fairly universal, and incredibly damaging, but absolutely possible to eliminate.

The best way to get started is to get the book and read it. The fable is compelling and entertaining and will likely strike an

---

* Here's the cool thing: Lencioni is so serious about helping all teams perform better that he created companion materials, such as *A Field Guide for Team Leaders, Managers and Facilitators* and a participant workbook, along with other tools that take all the guesswork out of the process.

immediate chord. I have yet to meet a leader who hasn't reacted with an "Oooh—that sounds kind of like my team" once they've begun reading the book.

WHAT TO DO ONCE YOU'VE READ *THE FIVE DYSFUNCTIONS OF A TEAM*

THE SIMPLEST—AND MOST effective—way to begin the journey with your team is to do three things:

1. Order the book for each of your direct reports and make it required reading prior to getting together to discuss it.

2. Set aside two to four hours at your next offsite for your team to work through the first one or two activities in the workbook (the topics of trust and conflict).*

3. Establish a quarterly cadence of spending a couple of hours as a team to continue working through the activities in the workbook. Some teams prefer to condense the process into a couple of months, devoting time at a monthly meeting to tackling one of the five dysfunctions, until they have gone through the entire workbook. Either approach is fine. The important thing is to actually *do the work as a team* ... and that requires time and prioritization.

---

* You don't need to bring in an external facilitator for this, but you can if you like. I have found the workbook to be so intuitive that my team didn't need someone else to help us through it. However, other teams I've worked with loved having a third party facilitate the conversations and exercises so that both the team leader and team members could relax and participate fully.

THREE "WATCH-OUTS"—EXCUSES, MESSINESS, AND DENIAL

MANY LEADERS WILL immediately react to my proposal here by saying, "Oh, my team isn't that bad. And besides we are too senior for something like this." Or "We've done team building before and it was a waste of time and money." Or "This is just hocus-pocus HR stuff that distracts us from our real work." I'm sure you could come up with all sorts of excuses for *not* taking your team on this journey from dysfunction to high function.

My experience is that the leaders who have all the excuses for why it won't work are the least effective leaders among their peers and the most likely to have the largest blind spots about their own leadership impact.

Then there's the issue of individual or collective discomfort— the inherent messiness of going through a process like this. I mean *emotional* messiness. The kind of messiness that makes people want to "turtle" or run for cover.

This emotional messiness is a natural part of the process. Anytime you take a group of human beings and start deliberately focusing on increasing trust, breaking down unhelpful barriers, and creating conditions for healthier conflict to occur, emotions will be front and center. And that's good.

It's not always comfortable in the moment, but it is worthwhile work and you will come to a better place on the other side. The reason I value Lencioni's approach so much is that the process and activities are always in pursuit of operating as a better team *in order to deliver better business results.*

This is not about sitting in a circle, holding hands, and singing "Kumbaya." It's about creating a team that consistently overdelivers in a way that feels good to all involved.

The final "watch out" is the river of denial that some of your direct reports may be floating down. There are usually one or two naysayers in every team who try to minimize the value or importance of this journey.

There may be sly comments like, "Gosh, boss, do we really have time to devote two hours to our team dynamics when we are trying to close the quarter?" or "Wow, sure seems like we are spending a lot of time talking about feelings, but I don't really see what difference it is making."

These types of "I'm just being rational" comments are usually from those team members whom everyone else finds most difficult to work with. That is, frequently, the person causing the most trouble to the team is the source of the subtle or not-so-subtle resistance to working on team dynamics.

Don't fall for it. This is a moment where you can just calmly reply, "Now is the time to get on the bus, Gus." In other words, don't put up with it.

IT'S UP TO YOU NOW

CONSISTENTLY HIGH-PERFORMING TEAMS that really love and care for one another (yes, I used the word "love"—it *is* possible to adore the people you work with) don't just happen.

It takes *intention* by the leader.

And it takes the team members being *all* in.

So, are you serious about transforming how your team operates? I've just given you the tools that have worked over and over—not just for the teams I've led but for numerous other teams I've seen go on this journey as well. It's up to you now.

You don't need to develop your own plan or spend thousands of dollars on an expensive coach or consulting firm. Don't overcomplicate this. Buy Lencioni's book, read it, and get started.

PS. Did I mention that the process is fun and your team will end up enjoying it and likely love you even more for doing it?

32

How to Lead a Big Change Program (*Psst*–It Isn't Business as Usual)

I HAVE A WOODEN paddle hanging in my office that I absolutely cherish. One side is emblazoned with the signatures of the best team members I have ever led. They gifted me this paddle when I left Jim Beam, after we had worked together for four and a half wild and crazy years. On the other side of the paddle is the phrase "NOT BAU," which stands for "Not business as usual."

I love this paddle because it acknowledges one of the big moments we shared as a team—and it was not a pleasant one. This "moment" entailed a verbal spanking of my team to get its attention—a spanking that none of us will ever forget.

My faults as a leader led up to this verbal spanking. We were several months into a massive efficiency and effectiveness transformation for our function—that's code for reducing headcount dramatically, restructuring the entire function, and increasing impact and service to our customers—all while doing our "day jobs."

This project spanned 18 months and radically changed every-thing we did and how we did it. Certainly, the very definition of a big "change program."

It was the number one priority after taking care of our cus-tomers. Yet every time we discussed the project, my team of generously paid vice presidents was disjointed—these VPs weren't communicating with one another, and didn't seem to share my sense of urgency. After a particularly disappointing team meeting, I shared my frustrations with my coach, Michael Hall.* He asked me how I was managing my team differently given that this wasn't "business as usual."

The answer? I wasn't.

And that was my mistake.

So I sat back and reevaluated how I was leading the team given that we were operating in a *"not* business as usual" con-text. I channeled all my frustration and irritation of the previous several months into a "come to Jesus" speech that I bracingly delivered to my stunned team the next morning.

The reaction to my "this-is-NOT-BAU-folks-and-we-are-going-to-start-acting-like-it" speech, where I openly shared how upset I was, my disappointment in their lack of communication with one another, and my determination that we were going to get our act together and "start doing things differently around here" struck a nerve with everyone.

There was a spectrum of responses. Two of my direct reports immediately said words to the effect of "Sorry, boss. You're right. I'm on board, so let me know how I can lead from the front more, and I will start proactively reaching out to my peers to solve

---

* If you've read Part 1, "You First," you know about Michael Hall. He is the brilliant founder and CEO of WildWorks, a business and leadership consultancy based in Sydney, Australia.

issues before they get to you." At the other end of the spectrum was this response: "How dare you speak to me that way, I'm a vice president!" (As you can imagine, the person who said that didn't last much longer on the team.)

But the most significant reaction came three days later from one of my highest performers. She sat down in my office and said she went home the night of my NOT BAU speech very angry with me. As she relayed what I had said to her husband, expressing her frustration at my lack of acknowledgment of how hard she was already working, her husband asked her, "But are you working on the right things? I think that's Mindy's point."

And that's when she got it. She admitted that she hadn't been treating the change program as her number one priority but instead spent all her time doing her "day job" and then tacking the change-program work on to the end. She had failed to reprioritize not only her work but also her team's work.

> Not only do you need to *talk* the NOT BAU talk (meaning communicate, communicate, communicate), you need to *walk* the NOT BAU walk.

While I was deeply grateful for her mature response, introspection, and insight (and it wasn't just her—she was representative of her peers as well), I was sobered by my leadership failures.

Although I had had kickoff meetings and communicated that the project was a priority, and we had a solid project plan, I had not communicated that we were operating (and would be for almost two years) in a different way.

It was my job to establish a NOT BAU operating rhythm. To not only change how I was scheduling and prioritizing my time but to explicitly direct my team to do so also.

HOW TO DRIVE A SUCCESSFUL CHANGE PROGRAM

HERE'S THE KEY principle to driving a successful change program that doesn't result in a paddling:

Lead from the front.

You are in charge. You get paid to be in charge. Act like it. As you go, so goes the team.

What does that really mean in practical terms?

Not only do you need to *talk* the NOT BAU talk (meaning communicate, communicate, communicate), you need to *walk* the NOT BAU walk. I am going to assume you have an excellent project plan for your big change program, with measures, deliverables, deadlines, and so on. It is what you do with that plan and how you lead your team that is the point here.

Here's what I mean by walking the NOT BAU walk:

- *Tangibly demonstrate how your schedule is changing to accommodate the change program.* For instance, show that this is a new era by publishing a 12-month calendar that illustrates how you are changing your own schedule to support this number one priority.

- *Communicate that your meetings associated with the change program are report-out meetings and sacred.* Make any meetings associated with the change program nonnegotiable must-attend forums, whether biweekly, monthly, or quarterly. Reinforce that they are report-out forums where your team will share its progress with you. It is in these sessions that any previously unsolvable issues will be elevated, debated, and resolved, with your involvement.

- *Direct your team members to establish a meeting cadence with their peers and teams.* These meetings are to be nonnegotiable, so that your team members are prepared and don't embarrass themselves at your report-out meetings.

- *Reschedule, reduce, or eliminate routine BAU meetings.* If you are really serious about the change program being a number one priority, you must create space in everyone's calendar, including your own. Let me repeat: you *must* create the space for people to do the work—don't just pile it on.

- *Delegate greater authority to your team.* Expect your direct reports to step up and address matters you would commonly get involved with.

- *Reestablish behavioral norms.* For example, lay out the clear expectation that your team must proactively work together to resolve issues before bringing them to you.

- *Provide broader communications.* With the help of our partners at WildWorks, we created a monthly, interactive Web-based email newsletter that I distributed to our global function, as well as to our CEO and executive team. In a fun visual way, the newsletter highlighted progress on the change program. It also called out great accomplishments from various team members and groups that had overcome obstacles to beat deadlines or deliver a terrific solution.

- *Publicly and privately reinforce the authority of your leadership team.* Every chance you get, support your direct reports (whether formally or informally) so they know and everyone else knows that you support them as they lead from the front.

- *Involve your boss.* Engage your boss in recognizing your direct reports for their dedication, commitment, and perseverance. In my case, we had a seminal meeting with my boss—the CEO—where my direct reports shared their commitment to our change program (which involved an audacious reduction in headcount while increasing customer service effectiveness, all while making the transition smooth and indistinguishable to the organization, on a crazy-fast timeline) and how they were approaching it. There were no PowerPoint decks or presentations, just an informal dialogue among leaders. We had this type of meeting three times throughout the 18 months, and my team felt so valued and fired up that the CEO cared enough to spend his valuable time discussing what they were working on and his perspective on their progress. Tailor the recognition to what will encourage and engage your team the most. For my crew, time with the CEO was the ultimate.

> **Tailor recognition of your team to what will encourage and engage the team the most.**

MY TEAM ULTIMATELY achieved the almost unachievable. I am still proud of them. When they teasingly presented me with the NOT BAU paddle at my going-away party (which was a couple of years after the change program was complete), they told me that that NOT BAU meeting was one of their greatest turning points as a group.

I am not advocating the type of moment that occurred in my NOT BAU meeting unless it's absolutely necessary. Ideally, it won't come to that. But if it *is* necessary, you must have the courage to do it. To course correct. To lead differently.

More importantly, by applying the principles outlined in this chapter, a "come to Jesus" meeting will never be needed because your team will be clear that you are driving big change, which is most certainly *not* business as usual.

33

Meeting Management Made Easy

ONCE SPOKE WITH the CEO of a major international airline about the operating cadence he had established with his executive team when he took the job. He had simplified the reporting process of his P&L and functional leaders, and his approach was something like this:

- Monthly market updates by the business leaders in writing (bullet pointed and no more than one page) on numbers delivery, what was working in market, and challenges.

- Quarterly business review meetings with the entire executive team and the line leaders.

- Quarterly offsite strategic meetings with the executive team to discuss longer-range planning, talent, and other higher-order items.

That's it.

I love the clarity of this CEO's operating cadence on both his role ("I'm the CEO, not a line manager") and that of his executive team. We both understood how annoying it is for a P&L leader to be burdened and distracted by too many meetings.

Meetings are the bane of a business professional's existence. Too many meetings. Running from meeting to meeting. Poorly run meetings. There are dozens of books covering all aspects of business meetings, everything from what kind of doughnuts should be offered to what prayers can be said. Of course, there's also a large category of books and other media on how to eliminate useless meetings, or even all meetings whatsoever. Jeff Weiner, CEO of LinkedIn, embraces this quest.*

> **Always devote time during a monthly meeting to look ahead 30, 60, and 90 days so that your team can anticipate and plan accordingly.**

My purpose here is not to add to the literature on this most hated of topics but simply to offer a few ideas on common frustrations. If you ever figure out how to run a business without meetings, please let me know. Meanwhile, for those of you with little time but immediate need, read on.

---

* Jeff Weiner, "A Simple Rule to Eliminate Useless Meetings," *LinkedIn Pulse*, July 2013.

MEETINGS MADE EASIER: SOLUTIONS TO COMMON ISSUES

ISSUE	SOLUTION
Lackluster engagement by team members at team meetings. (Corollary: leader doing all the work.)	**ROTATE OWNERSHIP OF THE AGENDA** I first experienced this when sitting on a regional leadership team in Asia-Pacific. My boss, the leader of a $1.5 billion business, had a schedule for the entire year published, putting the names of all the team members against the monthly business review meetings on a rotational basis. When our month came, our job was to grab the notes and action items with updates from the previous month, send them out to the team with a request for agenda items, and then on the day of the meeting, run the meeting, write the minutes, and send them out afterward. Believe me, everyone on the team was highly engaged in both the content and the process, and our boss wasn't running around like a headless chicken trying to do all the "administrivia" associated with quality meeting management. I have since employed this model with every team I've led, and it always works like a charm.
Geographically dispersed team struggles to agree on common solutions to common issues.	**BLITZ THE WORK** When you need to get things done, bring your team together (or whoever needs to be involved) in one room and set aggressive goals on actually accomplishing real work during the meeting. I typically say something low-key like, "None of us are leaving this room until we get X accomplished." (Funny how motivating that is.) I call this the SWAT-team approach. I've found it incredibly useful when leading a geographically dispersed team that gets together only a couple of times a year. To ensure that everyone is aligned and has ownership of the work, it is critical to have them participate in creating the work (I call this baking the cake). Otherwise they will proceed to reject any solution that is delivered from corporate, or waste time and money coming up with their own solution (baking their own cake) when it is unnecessary. Remove that temptation by using those periodic offsites to get actual work done—as opposed to just planning it.

Team in "fire-fighting" mode due to constant surprises.	**LOOK AHEAD** Always devote time during a monthly meeting to look ahead 30, 60, and 90 days so that your team can anticipate and plan accordingly. Spend time discussing possible risks and derailers. Assume the worst-case scenario and include steps in your plan to mitigate it. This sounds simple, but it is often overlooked. Teams can get caught up in the day-to-day and lose sight of anticipating what's next in the near term.
Team haphazardly laying out strategic plans that lack quality thinking.	**LOOK EVEN FARTHER AHEAD** The principle of looking ahead holds for quarterly meetings also. Ensure that you are constantly anticipating what is to come on a rolling four-quarter basis. Begin to build a discipline of thinking longer term about your business or department and having that inform your daily or monthly decisions. This capability will make it easier for your team to think strategically when the time comes.
Team repeatedly makes the same mistakes.	**LOOK BACK... AND LEARN** One of the biggest mistakes we make in business is failing to reflect on what we've learned the past year, the past quarter, or the past month. Make sure to pause with your team and ask, "What have we learned in the past X months?" or "What do we know to be true today that we didn't know before?" Gather everyone's answers and then move into a discussion on how to apply that insight to current and future effort.

These solutions to these five common issues are simple to understand, but discipline is required on your part to ensure that they are consistently implemented and become habitual for your team. If they do, the end result may even be *fewer* meetings (hallelujah!). At the very least, your meetings will no longer be useless.

34

Putting It All Together: Leading Your Team

LEADING A TEAM has been one of the greatest pleasures of my business career—though it may have been less pleasurable for some of my team members as I stumbled along the learning curve!

And that's the thing. There is no arrival point. The learning curve will always be there. As a leader, you will always be perfectly imperfect. It takes courage to acknowledge that fact, and it takes courage to lead. The key is to continue to improve and to care about improving, rather than thinking, "I'm good enough as it is. They all just need to adjust to me."

Let's recap. In this section, you learned:

1. How to accelerate team performance while reducing the anxiety and uncertainty connected to a new boss, by sharing your Personal Declaration and conducting a New Leader Assimilation session.

2. How to use monthly 1:1 meetings with your direct reports to massively increase your leadership effectiveness and their level of engagement and trust while also tackling tough development areas in a stress-free manner.

3. How to get the right people into the right roles by using the best hiring methodology.

4. How to shift your mindset so that terminating someone for poor performance doesn't suck the life out of you.

5. How to build a rock-star team whether you have individual rock stars or not.

6. How to walk the NOT BAU ("not business as usual") walk by adopting nine proven behaviors that will ensure you are successful as you lead a large change program.

7. How to ensure effective meeting management by implementing practical solutions to common issues.

When it comes to the topic of team leadership, this book is clearly not exhaustive. The tips, tools, and advice offered in these pages are all based on three enduring principles:

Principle 1: *People join companies and leave managers . . . and to be an effective leader, you need to care about this.*

Principle 2: *Servant leadership is the name of the game, and that means treating the people who work for you as you would want to be treated.*

Principle 3: *Keep it real and keep your sense of humor. If all else fails, simply focus on not being a jerk as a leader.*

Nothing is more uplifting than working with a group of people whom you love and respect. And when that respect is mutual and you are a valued truth teller, you will be blessed with some of the best relationships of your professional life.

MY READING
RECOMMENDATIONS

TO HELP YOU discover more about yourself and what drives you, spend some time with these four books:

- *StrengthsFinder 2.0* by Tom Rath. This quick read will help you uncover your top five strengths.

- *What Got You Here Won't Get You There* by Marshall Goldsmith. The title says it all. This is a book that requires you to be courageous with yourself and to tell yourself the truth, but it is oh so worth it!

- *The 7 Habits of Highly Effective People* by Stephen R. Covey. There is a reason this book is considered one of the best leadership books of all time and has sold over 15 million copies worldwide.

- *The Passion Test* by Janet Bray Attwood and Chris Attwood. This book lays out a powerful method for getting clear on what you really want your life to look like and what your true passions are.

And don't forget to check out these three stellar books on team leadership:

- *Who: The A Method for Hiring* by Geoff Smart and Randy Street

- *The Five Dysfunctions of a Team* by Patrick Lencioni

- *Monday Morning Leadership* by David Cottrell

ACKNOWLEDGMENTS

THERE ARE THREE people who believed in me from the moment I declared I was leaving my corporate life behind to write this book for the "corporate tribe" I adore: my son, my mother, and my soul mate. Thank you for your constant encouragement, love, and support.

My personal pit crew has been my lifeline for years. My heartfelt gratitude goes first and foremost to my dearest friend, advisor, and all-around miracle worker, Dr. John Sinnott. John—I wouldn't be where I am in my life without you!

Karin Fink and Prue Trollope—thank you for being the best girlfriends ever!

Ann Hackett is not just part of my pit crew but is also my mentor and inspiration. Thank you, Ann, for showing me that you can live wholeheartedly in the corporate world and for role modeling what true success looks like.

My gratitude to the ever-amazing and insightful Michael Hall, the brilliant Gisela Falstein, and the entire team at Wild-Works. Your partnership, advocacy, friendship, and coaching have been priceless.

Mike Hyter, thank you for believing in me when I was a "junior burger" at Walmart, and for all your encouragement, support, and, most of all, friendship all the years since.

The catalyst to moving *The Courage Solution* from concept to reality was the entire October 2014 Enlightened Bestseller crew. Thanks especially to Geoff Affleck, Chris Attwood, Janet Bray Attwood, Joel Roberts, Jennifer Scavina, Marci Shimoff, and Chrissie VanWormer.

I owe a huge debt of gratitude to the teachings and leadership philosophies of Sam Walton and Doug Conant, along with the authors and thought leaders I have referenced throughout this book, notably: Dr. Brené Brown, David Cottrell, Stephen Covey, Dr. Paul Eccher, Marshall Goldsmith, Patrick Lencioni, Tom Rath, Geoff Smart, and Randy Street—your ideas rock!

I've had some incredible bosses throughout my career but learned the most from Mark Alexander, Jeff Byrne, Johnnie Dobbs, Nancy Reardon, Lewis Rusen, and Matt Shattock. Thank you.

As I wrote the "Lead Your Peers" section of this book I was reminded again and again how lucky I was to work on leadership teams with the following superstars: Albert Baladi, Shelley Carlin, Jacqueline Chow, Nick Fink, Craig Funnell, Kevin George, Steve Graham, Doug Klie, Stacey Mason, Michael Moeller, John Montgomery, Simon Moran, Bob Morrissey, Lorraine Murphy, Bill Newlands, John Owen, Bob Probst, Andy Ridler, Kent Rose, Don Shanin, Trevor Stevens, and Paul Williams.

It is impossible to write about how to lead a team effectively without thinking about all the talented people I've been blessed to have as colleagues. The entire list would be too long to share here, so I want to particularly thank the following folks, who at one time or another (or at many times) were direct reports of mine and from whom I have learned so many valuable lessons: Cheryl Allen, Fran Bruno, Gary Beikoff, Frank Cortese, Paula Erickson, Sue Gannon, Graeme Hunter, Evelyn Jackson, Toni

Jones, Libby McElroy, Shelle Mitchell, Dan Perryman, Aaron Quinn, Matthew Saxon, Craig Shand, Steve Silver, Larry Smith, Tom Strehle, and Jim Tighe. Thank you from the bottom of my heart—I have loved working with each one of you!

Immense gratitude to Jesse Finkelstein and the entire Page Two team, along with Adrienne Fontaine, David Hahn, Emily Labes, Judy Phillips, Matt Rees, Mitch Sisskind, and Josie Urwin, for their incredible talent, advice, and support in getting this book published. Thank you!

And finally, thank you to my sister and brother. We started this life journey together, and we are still here and relatively sane! I love you both more than you know.

ABOUT THE AUTHOR

MINDY MACKENZIE—or the "Velvet Hammer," as she was known during her days at liquor giant Jim Beam—is a sought-after speaker and CEO advisor to Fortune 100 companies. Her passion is inspiring business professionals to increase their personal fulfillment through dramatically improving their professional impact.

Mindy served as chief performance officer of Beam, Inc., where she was responsible for a team of 150 and was part of the executive team that led consistent outperformance and created tremendous shareholder value, delivering double-digit earnings growth. It was her ability to lead her executive team colleagues in a refreshing "truth-telling" manner while maintaining her professionalism and grace that earned her the aforementioned nickname. Ultimately, Mindy led the organizational negotiations for the $16 billion dollar buyout of Beam, Inc. by the large Japanese holding company Suntory. Mindy's impressive career also includes five years at Campbell Soup Company and nine years at Walmart, where she advanced through various senior leadership HR and organizational development roles.

Mindy currently serves as a senior advisor for McKinsey, one of the most prestigious management and consulting firms in the world. She is a frequent guest lecturer for the MBA and Executive Education programs at Kellogg School of Management at Northwestern University. Mindy holds a bachelor's degree from Ambassador University and a master's degree from the University of Louisiana. Mindy lives with her son in the Chicagoland area.